Maurer, Warren R

Gerhart Hauptmann

DATE DUE			

Gerhart Hauptmann

Twayne's World Authors Series

Ulrich Weisstein, Editor of German Literature

Indiana University

TWAS 670

GERHART HAUPTMANN
Etching by Emil Orlik, 1922

Gerhart Hauptmann

By Warren R. Maurer

University of Kansas

Twayne Publishers • *Boston*

To Elizabeth
and Stephen

Gerhart Hauptmann

Warren R. Maurer

Copyright © 1982 by G.K. Hall & Company
All Rights Reserved
Published by Twayne Publishers
A Division of G. K. Hall & Company
70 Lincoln Street
Boston, Massachusetts 02111

Book Production by Marne B. Sultz

Book Design by Barbara Anderson

Printed on permanent/durable acid-free
paper and bound in the United States of
America.

**Library of Congress Cataloging in
Publication Data**

Maurer, Warren R.
Gerhart Hauptmann.

(Twayne's world author series; TWAS 670)
Bibliography: p. 146
Includes index.
1. Hauptmann, Gerhart, 1862–1946—
Criticism and interpretation.
I. Series.
PT2616.Z9M36 1982 832'.8 82-9358
ISBN 0-8057-6517-4

Contents

About the Author

Warren R. Maurer has been a professor of German in the Department of Germanic Languages and Literature at the University of Kansas since 1968. He has also served as chairman of that department and held teaching positions at the University of California (Berkeley) and at Indiana University. Born in Pennsylvania, he holds degrees from Franklin and Marshall College (B.A.), the University of Chicago (M.A.), and the University of California at Berkeley (Ph.D.), and has spent a number of years studying and working in Germany. Professor Maurer is the author of a book on German Naturalism, the co-editor of an anthology of articles on the poet R.M. Rilke, and the author of numerous articles on German literature, folklore, and onomastics.

Preface

Although it has long been a scholarly cliché that Gerhart Hauptmann wished to distance himself from the German Naturalist movement,[1] the chances that this will happen posthumously are more remote than ever. For nonspecialist readers and spectators in Germany, and for most literary critics and scholars in other countries, he is best remembered for perhaps a dozen dramas which, for all practical purposes, initiated a way of depicting reality with such felicity and intensity that its ramifications are still felt in the theater and cinema today.

Due to space limitations, the existence of a wide selection of recent studies of the movement,[2] and because a close examination of Hauptmann's work will make it largely redundant anyway, an extended discussion of German Naturalism here is neither possible nor necessary. Like others of his generation Hauptmann entered the scene when German literature, particularly drama, was in a period of stagnation, dominated, on the one hand, by such facile but popular French writers as Alexandre Dumas fils, Victorien Sardou, and Augustin Eugène Scribe, and, on the other, by a bland variety of epigones of German Classicism and Romanticism. The prevailing mood of this younger generation was one of injured national pride and the passionate desire for intellectual honesty, sincerity, and novelty. Gradually, especially during the 1880s, this same generation assimilated some of the "Naturalistic" tendencies perceived in such authors as the Frenchman Emile Zola, the Scandinavians Henrik Ibsen and August Strindberg, and the Russians Fëdor Dostoevski and Leo Tolstoy (*The Power of Darkness*). One latecomer to the movement, Arno Holz (together with his collaborator Johannes Schlaf), is chiefly responsible for the widespread but erroneous perception that German Naturalism is somehow consistent and unequivocal in its aims and outlook, and that it can be reduced to the attempt at achieving a photographic-phonographic accuracy in the reproduction of reality in art. Building on the idea of Zola's *roman expérimental,* Holz tried to put literary expression on a scientific basis in which the author would remain at least as detached from his materials as a chemist was from his. While his pseudoscientific terminology, such catchwords as *konsequenter Naturalismus* (referring to the "consequent" and total exclusion of an author's personality from his work) and *Sekundenstil* (a second-by-second recreation of reality), may strike us as quaint or nonsensical, they did significantly expand the parameters of the literary language of the day. His emphasis on the reproduction of every nuance and idiosyncrasy of human speech and gesture not only provided a new probe for the subconscious life of literary characters, but, more immediately and because natural speech is usually dialogue, led to a renewed emphasis on drama. Moreover, the very radicality of Holz's ideas, together with their attempted realization in such works as *Papa Hamlet* and *Die Familie Selicke,* gave impetus to a flagging movement and, most important from our perspective, helped Hauptmann discover his most congenial mode of expression.

Anyone approaching the task of surveying as prolific an author as Gerhart Hauptmann, for an audience not necessarily composed of literary specialists, will face a series of difficult choices. Should he try to deal with every work and fragment the author produced during a long lifetime—at the expense of being able to devote only a few paragraphs to each—or should he give a detailed analysis of a representative selection of works? Should he stress a broad historical background, or favor a more narrowly focused biographical approach for a writer known to depend heavily on personal experience for his creativity? Should he spend as much time on the poetry and prose of an author best known for drama, or should he exclude or slight these in favor of plays? Finally, should he give equal space to the works from all periods of an author's life, or concentrate on the works of those decades that are most widely known and that have found most universal acceptance? For the purposes at hand I have, in each instance, favored the second alternative.

As anyone who has been preoccupied with Hauptmann over a period of years will readily appreciate, the choice of which works to treat in some detail—at the expense of neglecting others—has not been an easy one. While the exclusion of the author's lyric poetry (e.g., *Das bunte Buch* [The Varicolored Book (1888)] and *Die Ährenlese* [approx. Gleanings (1939)]) will not strike many scholars as an unpardonable compromise in a general introduction of this kind, the neglect of such verse epics as *Der große Traum* [The Great Dream (written between 1914 and 1942)] or *Till Eulenspiegel* (1928) constitute omissions that the serious reader may wish to rectify with further reading on his own. Also to be recommended is a closer look at the prose works; especially the novels *Atlantis* (1912), *Phantom* (1922), *Die Insel der Großen Mutter* [The Island of the Great Mother (1924)], *Im Wirbel der Berufung* [In the Maelstrom of Vocation (1936)], *Der neue Christophorus* [The new Christophorus (a fragment)], and such shorter fiction as *Die Spitzhacke* [The Pickax (1931)], *Der Schuß im Park* [The Shot in the Park (1938)], *Das Märchen* [The Fairy Tale (1941)], and *Mignon* (1947). Even the area of drama, the genre with which this study is primarily concerned, would have benefitted from the treatment of numerous additional plays; e.g., comedies such as *Kollege Crampton* [Colleague Crampton (1892)], *Peter Brauer* (1910), and *Ulrich von Lichtenstein* (1939); historical and mythological dramas such as *Der arme Heinrich* [Poor Henry (1902)], *Kaiser Karls Geisel* [Charlemagne's Hostage (1907)], *Griselda* (1908), *Der Bogen des Odysseus* [The Bow of Odysseus (1912)], *Magnus Garbe* (written 1914–15), *Winterballade* [Winter Ballad (1916)], *Veland* (1925), *Die schwarze Maske* [The Black Mask (1930)], and *Hamlet in Wittenberg* (1935); as well as some additional plays in a Naturalistic vein such as *Christiane Lawrenz* (written 1905–7), *Dorothea Angermann* (1926), and *Herbert Engelmann* (1952).

Although I hope that even the experienced Hauptmann scholar may discover at least some new insights, my primary purpose here cannot be to reveal a new Hauptmann to old readers, but to introduce the prevailing Hauptmann to as many new readers as possible. For persons (including those who know no German) who wish to pursue their interest beyond an introductory level, I have provided a bibliography of translations and easily accessible secondary literature. (Here too I have had to be selective, favoring more recent studies and a somewhat disproportionately large number of items in English.) With the exception of some (by now generally accepted) titles, the translations from German in this book are my own.

It would be remiss not to express here my gratitude to the University of Kansas for a General Research Allocation grant and for a sabbatical leave for the academic year 1976–77, both of which greatly facilitated the work on this book, and to the editor of this series, Professor Ulrich Weisstein, for his patience and much helpful advice.

Warren R. Maurer

University of Kansas

Chronology

1862   November 15: Hauptmann born in Ober-Salzbrunn, Silesia.

1868   Begins attending village elementary school.

1874   Realschule am Zwinger in Breslau, where he attends school with his brother Carl (1858–1921).

1878   Agricultural trainee on estate of uncle in Lohnig and then Lederose; exposure to Herrnhut pietism.

1880   Admitted to sculpture class of the Königliche Kunst- und Gewerbeschule in Breslau.

1881   Writes *Liebesfrühling* for wedding of brother Georg (1853–1899); engagement to Marie Thienemann (1860–1914); begins work on *Germanen und Römer.*

1882   Leaves art school and, in the fall, begins one semester of study at the University of Jena.

1883   Mediterranean trip. October 1883 to March 1884 works as sculptor in Rome where he contracts typhoid fever; recovery and return home.

1884   Attends drawing class at Königliche Akademie in Dresden; studies at University of Berlin; work on *Promethidenlos* and *Das bunte Buch;* acting lessons.

1885   May 5: Marriage to Marie Thienemann; couple lives briefly in Berlin before moving to Erkner.

1886   Son Ivo born; extended visit to Putbus on island of Rügen.

1887   June 17: Speech on Georg Büchner before Berlin literary society *Durch;* witness at "Socialist Trial" in Breslau; son Eckart born; writes *Fasching* and *Bahnwärter Thiel.*

1888   Spring-fall: stay in Zürich with Carl and his family; psychiatric studies with Professor Forel; friendship with

Frank Wedekind; chance meeting with "nature apostle" Johannes Guttzeit.

1889 Son Klaus born in Erkner; Hauptmann meets fourteen-year-old Margarete Marschalk (1875–1957); October 20: turbulent premiere of *Vor Sonnenaufgang.*

1890 *Das Friendensfest; Der Apostel.*

1891 *Einsame Menschen;* meets Henrik Ibsen, Johannes Brahms, and Richard Strauss.

1892 *Kollege Crampton.* Public performance of *Die Weber* prevented by authorities.

1893 February 26: premiere of *Die Weber* under auspices of *Freie Bühne; Der Biberpelz; Hanneles Himmelfahrt;* close ties with Margarete Marschalk and beginning of Hauptmann's decade-long marriage crisis.

1894 Follows wife Marie and children to America; *Hannele* premieres in New York; renewed separation from his wife.

1896 *Florian Geyer;* Hauptmann awarded Grillparzer Prize for *Hannele;* Kaiser Wilhelm II prevents his receiving the Schiller Prize; *Die versunkene Glocke.*

1897 Trip to Italy with Margarete; intense dispute with brother Carl during Christmas season.

1898 *Fuhrmann Henschel.*

1899 Second Grillparzer Prize (for *Henschel*).

1900 *Schluck und Jau;* son Benvenuto born to Hauptmann and Margarete; *Michael Kramer.*

1901 Move into Haus Wiesenstein in Agnetendorf in the Riesengebirge with Margarete.

1902 *Der arme Heinrich.*

1903 *Rose Bernd;* Hauptmann ill.

1904 Divorce from Marie and marriage to Margarete; *Hirtenlied* fragment published.

1905   Awarded third Grillparzer Prize; *Elga;* honorary doctorate from Oxford University; visit to Stratford on Avon; meets George Bernard Shaw.

1906   *Und Pippa tanzt!*; infatuated with young actress Ida Orloff; meets Stanislavski.

1907   *Die Jungfern vom Bischofsberg;* long-awaited trip to Greece.

1908   *Kaiser Karls Geisel; Griechischer Frühling.*

1909   *Griselda;* honorary doctorate from University of Leipzig; lecture tour to Berlin, Vienna, Prague, Leipzig, Hamburg, Munich, and Zürich.

1910   *Der Narr in Christo Emanuel Quint.*

1911   *Die Ratten.*

1912   *Gabriel Schillings Flucht;* Nobel Prize for Literature; *Atlantis.*

1913   *Festspiel in deutschen Reimen* provokes nationalist opposition and is suppressed by order of the Crown Prince after eleven performances.

1914   *Der Bogen des Odysseus;* outbreak of World War I inspires Hauptmann to write nationalistic poems and newspaper articles.

1917   *Winterballade.*

1918   *Der Ketzer von Soana.*

1920   *Der weiße Heiland;* Rainer Maria Rilke participates in rehearsals.

1921   *Peter Brauer;* honorary doctorate from University of Prague; Hauptmann denies rumors that he is a candidate for *Reichspräsident.*

1922   *Indipohdi;* Hauptmann festival in Breslau and tumultuous 60th birthday celebration throughout Germany.

1923 Hauptmann and Thomas Mann spend fall vacation in same Italian hotel—impetus for Peeperkorn character in Mann's *Der Zauberberg.*

1924 *Die Insel der Großen Mutter.*

1925 *Veland.*

1926 Hauptmann reads from *Till Eulenspiegel* in the Reichstag; *Dorothea Angermann;* parts of *Mary* published.

1927 Hauptmann directs own version of Shakespeare's *Hamlet* in Dresden; *Die blaue Blume.*

1928 *Wanda; Till Eulenspiegel.*

1929 *Die schwarze Maske; Hexenritt.*

1931 *Die Spitzhacke.*

1932 *Vor Sonnenuntergang;* second (this time triumphal) trip to America.

1933 Advent of the Hitler regime; Hauptmann recedes from public life; *Die goldene Harfe.*

1934 *Das Meerwunder.*

1935 *Hamlet in Wittenberg.*

1936 *Im Wirbel der Berufung;* excerpts from *Der große Traum* published.

1937 *Das Abenteuer meiner Jugend.*

1939 *Tochter der Kathedrale; Ulrich von Lichtenstein; Ährenlese.*

1941 *Iphigenie in Delphi; Der Schuß im Park.*

1942 On Hauptmann's 80th birthday S. Fischer publishes the seventeen-volume *Gesammelte Werke,* including some previously unpublished items such as *Magnus Garbe.* Correspondence between Alfred Rosenberg and Goebbels concerning the Nazis' attitude toward Hauptmann.

1943 *Iphigenie in Aulis;* fragments of *Der neue Christophorus.*

1945   Trip to Dresden. Witnesses the destruction of that city on February 13.

1946   June 6: Hauptmann dies; buried on island of Hiddensee.

1947   *Die Finsternisse* published in New York: *Agamemnons Tod; Elektra; Mignon.*

1952   *Herbert Engelmann.*

Unless otherwise indicated, the above dates referring to Hauptmann's works indicate premieres (of dramas) and first printings.

Chapter One
Laurels and Roots

Fame and Reputation

If, prior to World War II, someone had inquired about Gerhart Hauptmann's status, the answer: "Germany's best-known and most important modern author," would have raised few eyebrows. Even more recently, one prominent German writer did not hesitate to pronounce him "the strongest literary force of our century."[1] While such esteem may puzzle a younger generation, it becomes more plausible on closer inspection.

The protean author of some fifty plays, twenty-five novels and shorter prose works, half a dozen verse epics, and numerous poems— not to mention an abundance of fragments, essays, speeches, diaries, and the like—Hauptmann saw his work popularized in movies and internationalized through translations into more than thirty languages. Nor was he denied appropriate critical attention. Between 1890 and 1950 almost every German critic concerned with literature and his own reputation seems to have felt compelled to comment on him, with the result that, by 1952, Hermann Weigand could claim that "more has been written about Hauptmann than about any other German author except Goethe; that to a wide and devoted following he came over many decades to be regarded as the incarnation of the poetic spirit. His appeal was broad, deep and lasting."[2]

Part of this appeal was, to be sure, a function of extra-literary qualities. Embodying much of the impressive humanity and disingenuous charisma of his caricature in the Mynheer Peeperkorn figure of Thomas Mann's *Magic Mountain,* people who knew him, especially in his later years, found him "majestic," "regal," or even a "prototype of man."[3] Although frequently controversial, Hauptmann was also strikingly sensitive to the subsurface cultural currents of his surroundings and became, through his best work, a veritable "seismograph of his time."[4]

1

If fame, fortune, and influence are considered appropriate tokens of esteem, the world was not niggardly in its rewards. The recipient of numerous literary awards, including the 1912 Nobel Prize, various honorary doctorates (the first in 1905 from Oxford), and the highest distinctions a grateful nation can bestow, Hauptmann enjoyed the rare privilege of seeing his work studied in the public schools and of having his birthdays celebrated as national events throughout Germany. Nor was this "king of the super-famous"[5] devoid of international appeal. His renown brought him into contact with numerous foreign luminaries, and his work served as an inspiration not only for fellow countrymen but for such disparate authors as Eugene O'Neill, James Joyce, and Anton Chekhov. Especially in Russia, where the first collected edition of his works appeared between 1902 and 1905, and where for a time he was that country's most popular dramatist, his influence was enormous.[6]

Perhaps the apogee of Hauptmann's popularity was reached in 1932 with the celebration of his seventieth birthday. In the fall of that year there were no fewer than 176 productions of his dramas on the stages of Germany, and his triumphal tour of the United States was, according to a reliable observer, the most tumultuous ever accorded a German in America.[7]

Curiously, by this time his strictly literary reputation was in decline. The turning point had come, according to various commentators, around 1912, 1913, 1918, or "during the time following World War I,"[8] and is associated with a departure from the more overtly Naturalistic techniques that characterized his most successful work.

During the intervening years this erosion of critical esteem has been exacerbated by a number of factors. Possibly because of a somewhat meagre formal education combined with a highly eclectic mentality, and certainly because of his status and rather finely honed commercial instincts, he was tempted to publish work that was uneven (e.g., the novel *Atlantis* [1912] or just plain bad (e.g., the self-indulgent novel *Wanda* [1928]). That aspects of his work may appear antiquated today is a less serious accusation which can be leveled with as much justification against Ibsen, Shaw, or German Expressionism. To be sure, the metaphysical leanings of "this last German Classic,"[9] who put a premium on intuition and a seminal, noncerebral grasp of reality and the world, tended to run counter to a growing modern predilection for intellectual constructs, abstraction, or Marxist optimism regarding the enhancement of man's social and economic situation through agitprop. If, however, the term "modern" is more than just a synonym for "current" or "contemporary," if it includes also the genius to create timeless characters and situations with the power to affect present-day lives, Hauptmann remains as relevant for us as he was for his contemporaries.[10]

In order for an author to maintain an international reputation he must, of course, be readily accessible. Hauptmann, unfortunately, remains frustratingly untranslatable. As Lilian Furst has noted ". . . a translation is no guide to a Naturalist play. . . . Precisely because of the German achievement in the field of dramatic language, characteristic speech-patterns, dialectical coloring, verbal gestures, silences, etc., the problems of translation apply to German Naturalism more than to any other movement and largely account for its unwarranted neglect outside Germany."[11] Hauptmann, the most skillful German playwright to write in a Naturalistic vein, suffers most. Even German contemporaries were not always equipped to cope with the dialectal nuances of some of his works and, with the postwar Polonization of Silesia and a general leveling of language in East Germany, the dialects, constituting the very fabric of his best-known plays, are disappearing. The result is that more and more Germans themselves are confronted with productions of his dramas that are essentially "translated" approximations of the author's intentions.

The division of Germany is not the only political factor to have influenced Hauptmann's critical reception. From 1889 to the present there has never been a dearth of critics who, ignoring the author's protestations, have focused their attention on the real or imagined political overtones of his work. Marxists especially have found themselves in an ambiguous relationship to Hauptmann since, at times, he seemed to come tantalizingly close to embodying the ideals of a proletarian revolution only to veer suddenly into areas completely antithetical to their program.

More damaging to his personal (and therefore indirectly to his literary) reputation, was Hauptmann's failure to leave Germany during the Hitler era. In contrast to such famous emigrés as Thomas Mann, Alfred Döblin, and Bertolt Brecht, a decision to go into exile was not forced upon him by Nazi anti-Semitism or anti-Bolshevism. For

Hauptmann, a political *ingénu* with a lifelong tendency to vacillate and compromise, the test was a moral one; and, in retrospect, one may claim that, like so many of his compatriots, he failed it. The fact that he was already seventy years old in 1932, that he wished to be buried in native soil, and that he felt—rightly or wrongly—that emigration would hamper his work, may be considered mitigating circumstances by the generously inclined.

The above handicaps notwithstanding, Hauptmann scholarship continued to flourish after 1945, with special attention being given to the later works and to metaphysically oriented interpretations. Only during the last few years, in fact, has a debunking tendency again begun to make itself felt in political, psychological, or journalistic commentaries which slight Hauptmann the artist in favor of Hauptmann the (frequently fallible) man. Perhaps this too is not a totally negative development. For years some of his most influential critics were individuals with close personal ties to him; people who tended to speak of him in reverential tones which he did little to discourage. A reaction could be expected, and Hauptmann's overall stature is such that it can continue to bear honest dissent.

Because of the cliché that an author's work reflects his life (the New Critics spoke of a "biographical fallacy") it is difficult but necessary to plead a special case for Hauptmann. Not only did he write a number of works incorporating direct personal experiences almost painfully devoid of literary transformation, and others that skillfully conceal a basic autobiographical motivation, but, by his own admission, he "never wrote a line, which he did not experience in that way, or live through in a similar manner, or which was not in some connection autobiography."[12] As his lifelong publisher Samuel Fischer remarked in 1932: "Hauptmann, the man and his work, form a unity of rare legitimacy, they are completely identical"; to which a recent critic adds: 'Hauptmann didn't publish books, he published himself."[13]

Childhood Memories

Especially significant are the often traumatic experiences of childhood and youth, the years depicted in *Das Abenteuer meiner Jugend* [The Adventure of My Youth (1937)] This book gives us the best available insight into the development of Hauptmann the artist from the most unpromising beginnings to international renown, and may serve here as a brief introduction to those factors—familial, social, psychological, political and religious—that are indispensable to an appreciation of his work.

Gerhard *(sic)* Johann Robert Hauptmann was born around noon on Saturday, November 15, 1862, the fourth child of Robert (1824–1898) and Marie (Straehler) Hauptmann (1827–1906). Of his brothers and sister, the youngest, Carl (1858–1921), was four and a half years his senior while Johanna (1856–1943) and Georg (1853–1899) were too old to figure prominently in his childhood as playmates. Central to his early development was his birthplace, the hotel Zur Krone in Ober-Salzbrunn (Silesia). Taken over by Robert Hauptmann from his father and patriotically renamed by him Zur Preußischen Krone (Prussian Crown), its environs, its financial vicissitudes, and the obligations it imposed on its owners, had a lasting influence on Gerhart. Because, especially during the summer months, his parents were completely preoccupied with its operation, he was left to fend for himself, to wander freely about the premises and local countryside, with the result that he acquired very early a storehouse of experiences which were to stand him in good stead later. Direct cultural enrichment, to be sure, was minimal: access to a few adventure and fairy-tale books, an old piano for "improvisation" (later some violin lessons), the mysterious attraction of the local theater on the way to school, a cardboard Hamlet stage, and copies of the Sistine Madonna and of a Rembrandt painting on the walls of the hotel. More important were his observations of human nature. While it flourished, the Krone attracted German, Polish, and Russian nobility. Ivan Turgenev and a czarina had been guests; but, for the boy, it was the children of the rich who aroused his envy. Behind the façade of elegance, however, he soon discoverd a realm of sweat, stench, and drudgery. On the ground floor of the hotel were the kitchen, a *Bierstube* leased by an actor and frequented by less select members of society, and, more important, the cramped living quarters of drayman Krause and his family, where the local dialect was spoken, where Gerhart ate from a communal bowl, entertained the family's children with fairy tales of his own invention, and in general was treated like a son. These experiences were complemented by a host of other contacts: e.g., with impoverished weavers, on the one hand, and with nouveau riche peasants on the other, who, having become wealthy through the discovery of coal on their property, lavished money on such things as extravagant stables for their cattle while the miners in their employ barely eked out a living.

While the neglect of his parents contributed to a precocious social wisdom, it also had negative effects. Left in the hands of a superstitious nursemaid, Gerhart remembered mostly the painful beatings she administered, a fear of darkness and ghosts, and an "almost . . . cosmic sadness" (7:406).[14] A victim even then of oppressive dreams, he recalls how he dreamt of the earth rolling along in space and himself stuck to it "like a dizzy, condemned, minimal [speck of] life, in danger, at any moment, of plunging into endless space" (7:489). Lonely and tormented by feelings of inferiority, he compensated with an active imagination which occasionally led to deceptions and outbursts of sadistic violence—as when he participated in stoning a toad to a bloody mush (7:562).

Aggravating Gerhart's suffering was an intense dislike of school. Like many contemporaries, he could never adjust to the martial discipline and psychological and physical brutality of the Prussianized school system. And, while he had effortlessly absorbed a great deal of practical wisdom and nature lore from his surroundings, he was so petrified before his village schoolmaster Brendel ("wrath personified" [7:481]) that he could not learn anything. Indeed, he claims even to have learned to read by himself, using Daniel Defoe's *Robinson Crusoe* and James Fenimore Cooper's *Leatherstocking Tales* as congenial primers (7:495). Still, even school might have been palatable if he had had the understanding of his loved ones; but this too was not to be. His relationship to his brother Carl, who was much admired for his intellectual prowess, was largely that of an adversary. The boys shared a bedroom with their mother, competed for the affection of their parents, and frequently fought. On the way home from school Carl was in the habit of seizing Gerhart by the collar and marching him before him through the village streets like an arrested felon. Later, when Carl was seriously ill, it became plain what a superior position he enjoyed in his parents' affections, and Gerhart's childish question: "Has Carl died yet?" (7:657) is not without a certain ambiguous pathos.

Nor were the relationships of other family members conducive to a happy home life. Gerhart's mother, the daughter of a powerful, authoritarian local official, had married his father over the objections of her family and in spite of obvious areas of incompatibility. Robert Hauptmann, a fastidious, aloof man with aristocratic pretensions and a boundless admiration for Bismarck, found himself married to a Zinzendorff pietist who neglected her appearance and slaved long hours in the hotel kitchen while bemoaning her husband's spendthrift ways and shortcomings. Yet in spite of his mother's apparently subordinate position in the management of the hotel, it was in her that Gerhart saw the secret nucleus of the family. "It became clear to me," he wrote in retrospect, "that my entire childhood . . . stood under a matriarchy. In that the authority of my father, his position as leader and ruler, could change nothing" (7:682).

In 1874 Gerhart was sent off to school in Breslau with Carl—the beginning of a period of suffering which made his previous life seem idyllic. Here he lived with his brother and some thirty other students in a flea-and-lice-infested boarding house; continued his humiliation in school (aptly named *Zwinger* ["dungeon"]); and looked forward only to the vacations when he could pour out his troubles to his mother. To be sure, his life brightened somewhat when he moved into the more pleasant household of an older prison pastor and his very young wife. Here he found moments of release among the family's children whom he entertained with hours of storytelling, but school remained a traumatic burden and his only other pleasant moments seem to have centered on the discovery of a number of German authors (notably Adalbert von Chamisso, Johann Gottfried Herder, Friedrich Hölderlin, and Novalis), and the visit to Breslau in 1876–77 of the famous Meiningen theater troupe with performances of *Julius Caesar, Macbeth,* Friedrich von Schiller's *Wallenstein* and *Wilhelm Tell,* and Heinrich von Kleist's *Hermannsschlacht* [Battle of Arminius]. Gerhart's first literary efforts—some melancholy poetry and a dramatic fragment in the *Tell* mode *(Konradin)*—date from about this time.

Having distinguished himself only in failure, he left the *Zwinger* in 1878 in order to accept an offer of his aunt and uncle, Julie and Gustav Schubert, to live with them as an agricultural trainee, first on an estate in Lohnig and then in nearby Lederose. While happy to escape school, the youth soon discovered that he had made yet another mistake. The endless round of exhausting work; the suffocating pietistic atmosphere; the burden of unenlightened puberty (whose "sins" he equated with religious damnation); a weakened constitution; the fire-and-brimstone sermons of itinerant lay preachers—all these brought him to the brink of a religious mania from which he was only saved by a visit home and the refreshing rationalism of brother Carl and his friend, a young man named Alfred Ploetz. Although he did not know it at the time, the Schubert interlude turned out to be valuable later. It gave him a profound understanding of rural life, religious sects, and the New Testament; showed him that the impoverished peasants had no sympathy for the German nationalism he had so blindly accepted until then; gave him some time for poetry and sketching; and, through his Aunt Julie and her piano, provided some lasting musical enrichment.

Art and the Germanic Past

Having added agriculture to his list of failures, Gerhart returned to Breslau to study. A high point of this period was a surprise initiation into a secret *Blutsbrüderschaft* ("blood brotherhood") consisting of Carl, Ploetz, and several friends, with the Pan-Germanic aim of uniting all Germanic tribes and nations. Inspired by the spiritual preceptors of the group, the popular historical authors Felix Dahn and Wilhelm Jordan, Gerhart wrote a dramatic fragment, *Frithiofs Brautwerbung* [Frithiof's Courtship (1879)] and an alliterative *Hermannslied* [Lay of Hermann (1880)] in imitation of their work. A passionate love for a robust country girl, Anna Grundmann, whom he met on a vacation trip back to Lederose, had convinced him that quick literary fame was his best chance for winning her. Unfortunately, his jealous uncle intercepted his letter of proposal and the romance faded.

It is an indication of the young Hauptmann's vacillation at this time that an artist acquaintance of his father, whom he met in the summer of 1880, could inspire him to change his intense literary ambitions to an equally strong interest in the plastic arts. With the blessings of his father (his mother thought he should become a gardener), he managed to be admitted to a sculpture class of the Breslau Königliche Kunst- und Gewerbe-Schule in October of 1880.

Although his work as a student sculptor remained traditional and derivative, his personality now underwent a metamorphosis. From a shy adolescent he became a proponent of nudism; took to spending his nights carousing (often in the company of James Marshall, a favorite professor); almost lost an eye in a brawl; and badly neglected his health and appearance. With shoulder-length blond hair and dimpled cheeks, even his sex seemed indeterminate and, before long, his dissolute life and inadequate support from home reduced him to penury. Under these conditions his studies naturally suffered, and one day he found himself expelled from art school for "bad behavior and insufficient industry and attendance" (7:804). Fortunately, a reading of his *Hermannslied* before a group of professors was so well received that it brought him not only a modicum of local fame but also gave his protectors, expecially Marshall and the sculptor Robert Haertel, sufficient cause to force a reinstatement, under the supervision of the latter in whose class he remained until April, 1882.

With his fortunes at a low ebb, there began a series of events which, perhaps more than anything else, influenced his future career. His brother Georg had met a young woman named Adele, one of five daughters of Berthold Thienemann, a rich businessman. Hauptmann's father was delighted with the find. "I tell you, a nest of birds of paradise!" (7:843) he is said to have exclaimed, and the "coincidence" that within a short time all three Hauptmann brothers had married Thienemann sisters can be explained as adequately on financial as on purely romantic grounds. Georg was the first to act. A week after the death of Herr Thienemann he and Adele announced their engagement—the wedding took place a year later, and in September, 1881, Gerhart wrote his *Liebesfrühling* [Spring of Love] for the celebration. At the wedding Gerhart and Marie Thienemann announced their engagement, repeating a step that brother Carl and sister Martha had taken half a year earlier. The engagement to Marie—more precisely the day when she discovered the extent of his hardship and gave him a handful of gold coins—marked a turning point. Henceforth he could travel, entertain and support friends, and devote himself to study and art.

Still vacillating between sculpture and writing, he dictated a drama *Germanen und Römer* [Germanic Tribes and Romans] to an "old unemployed gym teacher" (7:883) in August and September, 1882, and then, with the support of Haertel, managed to matriculate at the University of Jena. Here he occupied himself with two widely divergent fields of study: the materialist views of science and heredity as taught by Ernst Haeckel on the one hand, and the study of Plato and ancient Greece on the other. While he still maintained an interest in the Germanic past, the death of Richard Wagner in 1883 and a memorial service (including a performance of the last act of *Die Walküre*) which he attended in Weimar, convinced him that any further literary efforts in the vein of Dahn and Jordan—or of his own *Hermannslied* and *Germanen und Römer*—were futile. Wagner, he felt, had achieved a level of artistry in this area that could never be surpassed.

Travel Experiences

With his newly aroused passion for Greece providing the impetus (and his fiancée the funds), Hauptmann set out in April, 1883, on a Mediterranean cruise which took him to Malaga, Marseilles, Genoa, Naples, Capri, and Rome. His intention of reaching Greece was foiled by a meeting with Carl (also travelling on Thienemann money) in Genoa, and an ensuing dispute which led to an abrupt end to the trip. Highlights of the experience included nights spent aboard ship entertaining sailors with stories and emotional discussions; the initiation into the utter degradation of opium dens and child prostitution in Malaga; and the acquaintanceship with the bright daughter of a professor (which threatened to develop into a liaison) the details of which he dutifully reported to Marie upon his return.

His interest in sculpture having been renewed through the works of Michelangelo in Rome, he returned there in October of the same year and set himself up in the Via degli Incurabili as "Gherardo Hauptmann, Scultore" (7:956). With a Promethean confidence hardly justified by past achievement he spent some ten weeks of backbreaking labor on a statue of a colossal Germanic warrior only to see it—and his ambitions as a sculptor—collapse in a single tragicomic night. As if to complement his mental anguish, his body contracted typhoid fever, plunging him into a "splendid, holy" coma in which he felt "unspeakably well" (7:986) while actually hovering on the brink of death.

Breakthrough to a Literary Vocation

Upon recovery, Hauptmann made one more feeble attempt at a career in art by enrolling in a drawing class in Dresden but then moved on irrevocably to literature. Eighteen eighty-four found him in Berlin at work on his epic *Promethidenlos* [roughly, The Fate of the Children of Prometheus], which was inspired by his Mediterranean trip and which, in a Byronic vein, depicts the disillusionment and suicide of its hero, Selin; and on a book of poetry, *Das bunte Buch* [The Varicolored Book]. During this time he also discovered Ibsen and studied acting. The wedding to Marie (he preferred to call her Mary) took place on May 5, 1885, under circumstances that were less than auspicious. The groom cherished the view that man is by nature polygamous and was in such bad health that a witness speculated that he wouldn't live out the week.

After an abortive attempt to set up housekeeping in an apartment in Berlin (the noise and anxiety were conducive neither to his health nor to his young marriage), the couple moved to Erkner, a rural suburb of the colossal city. Here Hauptmann spent most of the next four years in pleasant natural surroundings, enjoying his family (including the birth, in quick succession, of three sons) and working hard at his craft. It was here too that he wrote the stories *Fasching* [Carnival], *Bahnwärter Thiel* [Flagman Thiel], and his first important play, *Vor Sonnenaufgang* [Before Daybreak]. He also occupied himself with studies on Jesus, continued writing poetry, began an autobiographical novel, and met a variety of people who served as models in such later works as the comedy *Der Biberpelz* [The Beaver Coat]. While still toying with the idea of a life in the theatre—as evidenced by a summer (1886) spent in Putbus on the island of Rügen with a troupe of actors—his ties to contemporary literature became stronger. He discovered an affinity to the zeitgeist embodied in Wilhelm Arent's *Moderne Dichtercharaktere;* established contact with the literary society *Durch,* where in a lecture and reading he introduced the then almost unknown Georg Büchner and became acquainted with Johannes Schlaf and Arno Holz, with whom, next to Hauptmann himself, the German Naturalist movement is most strongly identified.

He also found himself embroiled in the first of a series of political skirmishes which were to make life difficult for him in subsequent years. Called to Breslau in the summer of 1887 to testify in the *Sozialistenprozess* ("Socialist Trial") of the *Gesellschaft Pazifik* ("Pacific Society") consisting of a group of friends who had planned a utopian settlement in the United States, he, then as later, denied ever being a Socialist. "I always have my own views," he testified, "and therefore never share those of anyone else."[15]

The persecution of leftists in Bismarck's Prussia also led to a very fruitful stay in Switzerland during the summer of 1888. In Zürich he and Mary joined Carl and Martha and a small colony of German artists and scientists. In an atmosphere permeated by "faith, love, and hope" (7:1060) he made pilgrimages to Georg Büchner's grave, discovered Walt Whitman, and came under the influence of Professor Auguste Forel, the director of a local insane asylum. To the latter Hauptmann attributed profound psychological insights which helped him to portray characters, and the professor's strong views on female emancipation and the evils of alcohol are also reflected, if less permanently, in his own work. Notebook in hand, he also began studying the Salvation Army and the religious sects which the era produced in abundance, observed the first female university students, and even overstepped the bounds of friendship by recording the family squabbles of Frank Wedekind for later use. Speaking of Hauptmann's own literary efforts at this time, Wedekind remarked that he worked "like a steam engine."[16] The autobiographical novel he was writing contained depictions of his own sexual problems (an indication that all was not well in his marriage), and the discussions with Wedekind about sex led, according to Hauptmann, to Wedekind's successful drama *Frühlings Erwachen* [Spring's Awakening (7:1072)]. By this time he was himself making plans for a drama about the plight of Silesian weavers and had found his métier. Having turned from sculpture to writing and from imitation to a voice of his own, he decided to write about those things he knew best—the people and events familiar to him from his childhood and youth—and to exploit fully the dialect in which these memories returned to him.

Chapter Two
Early Prose

Fasching

In 1887, upon submitting *Fasching* for publication, Hauptmann requested that his first name be spelled Gerhar*t* (rather than Gerhar*d*), an orthography he retained for the rest of his life.[1] This minor change coincides with a much more significant change of aesthetic signature which was soon to lead to his most popular and enduring contribution: those many works that reflect an intimate amalgamation of personal experience, a vibrant sense of landscape, and warm portrayal of ordinary people confronted by forces and events too overwhelming to comprehend.

Due to the general disrepute of contemporary theater, combined with his attraction to Turgenev, Tolstoy, Zola, and Daudet,[2] Hauptmann turned to prose fiction and his first successful efforts in his new style were the novellas *Fasching* [Carnival] and *Bahnwärter Thiel* [Flagman Thiel]. While the former still bears traces of literary apprenticeship, the latter is an undisputed small masterpiece. Together they transcend Naturalism even before it reached its apogee and provide a more balanced insight into the future author than the more decidedly Naturalistic play *Vor Sonnenaufgang* which established his wider reputation in 1889.

Based on an actual event, the drowning of a shipbuilder named Zieb, his wife, and child, when they broke through the ice during a nocturnal crossing of the Flaken lake near Erkner on February 13, 1887, this story was long neglected, even after its rediscovery in 1922.[3] Using the event as a receptacle for his imagination and his emotions about the lake and the people around it, Hauptmann composed a somewhat contrived, melodramatic tale of hubris and death.

The plot is little more than an elaboration of the ironic title. After a dizzying round of celebrations, a man sets out for home, late at night, across a frozen lake. Skating on dangerous ice while pushing his wife and infant son before him on a hand sled, he loses his sense of direction when a dark cloud obscures the full moon and he is simultaneously deprived of the beacon of light from a lamp in his house upon which he had depended for orientation. Suddenly he finds himself plunged from a warmly animalistic enjoyment of life into the cold, dark waters of death in the one small portion of the large lake which had failed to freeze over completely. The next day all three bodies are fished from the lake and returned home, there to join in death the fourth member of the household, an old grandmother who, coincidentally, at about the same time, had died a natural death related to that of the others by the fateful lamp which had burned low because she could no longer attend to it.

Aside from the elemental depiction of the precariousness of human existence inherent in the central image of skating on thin ice, the story owes its effectiveness to the expressive characterization of its four principal characters, a demonization and estrangement of the natural surroundings, and a growing suspense maintained by an insistent foreshadowing of doom and an abundance of leitmotifs and effective visual and auditory imagery. The Zieb character, renamed Kielblock by Hauptmann in appropriate deference to his trade of sailmaker,[4] neglects his customers for the pleasures of carousing while, at the same time, speculating upon the death of his old mother whose strongbox full of savings—the result of a miserly lifetime—he hopes soon to acquire. His young wife Mariechen, instead of serving as a counterbalance to his excesses, is all too easily drawn into them herself. Her name, a diminutive form, suggests a lack of maturity which finds further expression in a favorite Hauptmann motif: child neglect and abuse. Far from considering him a blessing, the Kielblocks consider Gustavchen, their little son, a stroke of bad luck and a handicap to their preferred lifestyle. In Hauptmann's typology of characters Mariechen is also an early relative of those physically robust and erotically destructive women to whom he returned again and again.

Almost from the outset a mood of impending doom is evoked. It takes too many forms to be recounted in full here, but ranges from the very early description of Gustavchen's "death-like" sleep (6:16) to an incident in which Kielblock laughs off a fisherman's threat that he will have to fish him out of the lake in his net when he breaks through the ice (6:17); to his ridicule and parody of the cries of help of a boy who had almost drowned in the lake at the fateful spot in broad daylight (6:27)—cries later repeated almost verbatim in his own drowning (6:32). Especially evocative is Kielblock's behavior at a *Fasching* ball. Vaguely aware that a consciousness of death enhances the pleasure of living, he disguises himself as a corpse (whereas his wife, coquettishly attired in a red gardener᾿ ᾿ costume, represents life) and spends a few exuberant hours "teaching people the willies" (6:21).

As in *Bahnwärter Thiel*, albeit with less virtuosity, Hauptmann lavishes attention on the natural setting of his human drama. Nature goes its own way, hard and indifferent at best, malevolent and destructive at worst. The sun, a mere "piece of glowing metal" (6:24), and the moon a "silver knob" (6:28) observe with equal indifference the animal vitality and the death throes of the tiny human figures. As Kielblock struggles against drowning he is mocked by a flock of wild geese swimming effortlessly through the vast dome of stars and across the face of the full moon (6:32–33). More subjectively, the low "Tuba-call" of the cracking ice reminds him of standing upon "an enormous cage, in which hordes of bloodthirsty beasts are imprisoned, roaring from hunger and rage, and grinding their claws and teeth into the walls of their prison" (6:30). This is hardly the substance or language of "consistent Naturalism." Man is *a fated being,* an impression Hauptmann reinforces even in such subtle touches as the use of the same color (green) for the death-sled and the coveted strongbox. And, in spite of Naturalistic tendencies such as the accumulation of detail, the profuse use of dialogue (but sporadic and inconsistent use of dialect), and the *Sekundenstil* in which the moment of dying is recorded (6:33), the style is closer to magic realism—appropriate to the *aura magica* that the work exudes.

Bahnwärter Thiel

Reminiscent of *Fasching* in style and certain motifs (e.g., child neglect) is *Bahnwärter Thiel,* written in 1887 and published the following year in the Naturalist periodical *Die Gesellschaft.* With this work Hauptmann "entered the world as a writer" (7:1044) and gave German Naturalism one of its most accomplished and enduring works. Praised extravagantly by its first readers,[5] it has enjoyed long popularity in

German schools and in its motivation, psychological nuances, and form remains as fascinating today as on the day it appeared.

Again a product of life in Erkner, the character of Thiel seems to have been inspired by a railroad crossing guard who worked in that area.[6] The novella, of course, has more deeply personal roots as well. These undoubtedly include memories of railroad life acquired in Hauptmann's parents' railway restaurant; an early fascination with trains as an embodiment of the mixed blessings of technology (expressed also in the poems "Im Nachtzug" and "Der Wächter" ["In the Night Train" and "The Guard" (4:54–58)]; his attraction for Georg Büchner (7:1061); and an intense interest in psychology stimulated by Forel. For Hauptmann these elements began to coalesce after his "flight" to a new life in the "Waldeinsamkeit" ("forest solitude") of Erkner (7:1093): "I had never been so close to nature as then," he was to recall. "Through the mystery of birth [of a son] it was as though the earth too had opened itself up to me. The forests, lakes, meadows, and fields breathed within the same mystery" (7:1033).

Written in the early "hours before dawn,"[7] the novella relates the story of a large, seemingly phlegmatic and simple-minded crossing guard, Thiel, who is subjugated by two women: his first wife Minna, a delicate, ethereal creature who died in childbirth, leaving him to care for an equally vulnerable son Tobias; and an earthy, animalistic creature named Lene, whom he ostensibly marries to provide Tobias with a mother, whereas he actually does so for compulsive sexual reasons. Guilt-ridden by what he feels to be his betrayal of Minna, the stolid, punctilious anti-hero attempts to compartmentalize his life to accommodate two forms of love: accepting Lene's sexual domination during his off-duty hours at home but, simultaneously, transforming his little railway implement shack in the forest into a "chapel" where, with the help of quasi-religious relics of his dead wife, he achieves visionary states of communication with her. Thiel's attempts to keep the two areas of his life separated, however, are doomed to failure on account of little Tobias. Sickly, retarded, and undernourished though Tobias is, Thiel loves him as his link to Minna, thereby incurring the wrath of Lene who—veritable archetype of an evil stepmother—abuses the child at every opportunity and forces him to forgo the pleasures of childhood by burdening him with the responsibility of caring for her (and Thiel's) own infant son. Even though he accidentally witnesses a brutal beating of Tobias by Lene, Thiel's sexual bondage to her is so strong that he represses his rage and reverts to his usual torpor.

The crisis arrives in the aftermath of a mundane event. Given a small strip of land near his railroad shack for his private use, Thiel informs Lene of the fact without considering the consequences, i.e., the inevitable merging of the two realms he has so painstakingly kept apart. Having been told of the little field, Lene cannot be restrained from the urge to plant potatoes in it (a necessity, she claims, for the impoverished family) and one beautiful sunny morning finds the family heading for the fateful spot. At first the family's activity is a picture of idyllic harmony, impaired only by Lene's refusal to allow Tobias to accompany his father on his inspection round; she insists that he remain with her to care for his infant brother while she prepares the desolate little field for planting. As usual, her forcefulness prevails and suddenly tragedy strikes. Diverted by her work, Lene neglects to keep an eye on Tobias, as her husband had urged her to do, and the boy is brutally struck down by a raging locomotive. Efforts to save him by bringing him to the railway doctor prove futile. Thiel himself lapses into unconsciousness and then into a state of paranoia in which he promises revenge on Lene to his dead wife and catches himself in the act of strangling Lene's child. When the body of little Tobias is returned to the Thiel household a few hours later, Lene and her child are found dead; she with a shattered skull, the baby with a slashed throat. At first, Thiel, the murderer, cannot be located, but he is discovered the next day seated on the railway tracks at the scene of the accident, caressing the little brown cap of Tobias. An express train is made to halt while he is forcibly removed from the tracks. Taken to Berlin, he is eventually placed in an insane asylum.

Much of the original impact of this story must have resulted from its Naturalistic overtones. These include the depiction of a passive central character from a lower-class background in a specific milieu; problems of heredity (Tobias has his father's red hair but his mother's frailty and the mystical proclivities of both parents); emphasis on sexuality; the rather clinical description of mental derangement; a minutely detailed narrative style limited largely to a precise description of the few characters and their immediate environment; a preoccupation with the destructive forces of technology; the use of real place names, and the depiction of crass, almost sensational, reality (Lene's beating of Tobias,

Thiel's attempted strangulation of the infant, and the discovery of the mutilated bodies).[8] And yet, despite this impressive catalogue of attributes, even a first reading of the work reveals how inadequate the Naturalist label is. Compared to the "consistent" Naturalism of Holz and Schlaf, Hauptmann's novella is at once more traditional and more progressive, pointing to the past and to the future. An almost classical example of the novella genre as it flourished during the period of Poetic Realism, it also shares with that era a proclivity for describing in some detail the rudiments of a particular trade or occupation (here that of a railway flagman) without, however, placing it within the political context of a class-conscious proletariat.

Romantic elements also abound. Dreams become reality; natural surroundings are described subjectively so as to enhance the mystical experiences of the main character and to reflect his inner turmoil, while the language itself (e.g., in the use of the Romantic "code" word *Waldeinsamkeit* [6:47]) is, on occasion, almost indistinguishable from that of a Ludwig Tieck or Joseph von Eichendorff. Nor is this surprising in light of Hauptmann's lifelong latent Romanticism, detectable in even his most Naturalistic work. Indeed, it is largely these Romantic qualities that also tend to project the work into the future. Hauptmann's lack of faith in mere words as adequate vehicles of expression, his reliance on gesture, silence, symbolism, color imagery, the meaningful repetition of words and events, and an artistic control and fastidiousness second perhaps only to that of Thomas Mann, already point toward Neoromanticism.[9]

An important clue for locating *Thiel* more precisely in German literary history is provided by Hauptmann's admiration for Georg Büchner. Although Büchner had been almost a cult figure for him, and a few other Naturalists had instinctively recognized his relevance to their movement, his real discovery did not come until about 1911—just prior to the advent of Expressionism.[10] Although Büchner had died fifty years before *Thiel* was written, his work was still too progressive to be widely understood or appreciated. His drama *Woyzeck* and the novella *Lenz,* in particular, strike one as direct precursors of Hauptmann's work. Written in a similar style (a mixture of realism and symbolism), they represent two of the most sensitive analyses of mental aberration in German literature. The parallels between the hounded and abused soldier Woyzeck and Thiel are especially striking. As Silz has summed them up, "both are simple, not to say simple-minded, faithful, 'kinderlieb,' inarticulate, concealing profound spiritual depths beneath a usually tranquil surface; easy-going, slow to suspicion and wrath, but finally capable of murderous violence against the women who have failed them."[11] There are other similarities as well. Both men have a special relationship to nature and are subject to hallucinations; both are the victims of despotic, dehumanizing, materialistic "progress," both are obsessively attracted to women of robust sensuality, and, finally, both are spared the moral condemnation of their authors on the basis of a very similar outlook: that there are too many (and too obscure) determining forces acting upon human behavior to permit easy judgments.

In both *Woyzeck* and *Thiel* compassion for a poor, harassed individual from the lower classes far outweighs condemnation, and it is not surprising that both works have been the subject of Marxist-oriented criticism. Indeed, there are traces of a *j'accuse* tendency in *Thiel,* mostly in reference to little Tobias. For example, Hauptmann casually hints at his undernourishment in an episode in which the boy is described as using his finger to eat the lime from a hole in the wall (6:43). On the other hand, since Lene's own child is the picture of health, it would seem that this is more of a personal, family problem than a social one. More significant are some of the circumstances surrounding the accident. Inhumanely reduced to an object, "thrown to and fro like a rubber ball" (6:58) beneath the wheels of the train, Tobias's body is hurriedly wrapped up (in a red flag!) in the presence of the curious passengers: "Time is valuable. The whistle of the trainmaster trills. Coins rain from the windows. . . . 'The poor, poor, woman,' one hears in the compartments, 'the poor, poor mother' " (6:58). This confrontation of tragic loss with money, suffering with genteel banality, does seem to constitute a social statement—as does also the return of the boy's body in a gravel car (6:64). To try to impose the usual Marxist pattern upon the novella, however, to reduce Thiel's suffering to a catastrophe which "in the final analysis derives from the social problems of the hero," and to equate his religiosity with an "opiate of the people"[12] is, at best, an oversimplification. Even Irene Heerdegen, who broaches these views, seems aware of their limitation. On the one hand, she must regret that the work lacks a positive example for the proletariat and, on the other, admits that its basic orientation is more psychological than social.[13]

Psychological criticism of *Thiel* tends to fall into two categories: either features of the work itself are used to explore the psyche of the author, or the characters of the story are examined for psychological verisimilitude. An example of the former is Hauptmann's attraction to the theme of *mariage à trois*—typically a man between two women with contrasting natures and personalities. Whether or not one agrees with Jean Jofen that the third person in the triangle inevitably represents Marie Hauptmann, the author's mother (the name Minna is a diminutive form of her name), and therefore signifies oedipal complications, the theme is one that does occur again and again.[14] Similarly, the figure of Lene has been interpreted as a projection of Hauptmann's fear of sexually aggressive women during an era of pronounced feminine activism, and Tobias has been identified with the author's own childhood suffering.[15]

Less debatable is Hauptmann's skill in portraying the psychic life of his characters, especially of Thiel himself. Here we have a classic portrayal of repression avenged; of a man who bottles up both his sense of guilt and a growing rage beneath a pedantic orderliness. When, through the violent loss of his son, he is suddenly deprived of even the solace of hope for the future, it is more than he can endure. He loses his already tenuous hold on reality and his unconscious psyche wreaks vengeance on the world in a paroxysm of savagery that transcends mere revenge—reflecting instead a generous portion of self-loathing and " 'displaced' consciousness of his own guilt and perfidy."[16]

Bahnwärter Thiel is, of course, more than a sociological case history or the study of an interesting psychopath. Hauptmann takes pains to universalize his hero's fate; to make of him an Everyman trapped between the spiritual and the temporal realms. That Hauptmann's artistic vision cannot be completely divorced from either the zeitgeist or his own outlook should, however, be obvious. In his loneliness Thiel embodies both the growing alienation which was the by-product of an increasingly materialistic late-nineteenth century culture and the desperate longing for spiritual solace which was its concomitant reaction. In addition, he reflects the author's own, somewhat eclectic, philosophical notions. For example, Hauptmann once compared tragedy *"cum grano salis,* with a breakthrough of subterranean forces"
(7:101).

Whether or not these transcendental forces are benevolent or malicious, for Hauptmann, as for the ancient Greeks, they are a reality which reflects upon individual human destiny. Furthermore, like some Romantic thinkers he subscribes to the view that access to the transcendental realm is not only possible but that it is facilitated for certain individuals and under certain circumstances. In this regard, simple, primitive people living close to the soil are at an advantage, as the mysteries of existence, both divine and demonic, reveal themselves to them more directly than to their more highly civilized, excessively "rationalized" brethren. Especially in dreams, states of unconsciousness, and madness (frequently the result of great suffering) they acquire a foretaste of true being and, paradoxically, achieve their greatest clarity.[17]

Seen from this perspective, Thiel's life is "determined" not only in the scientific sense so dear to the Naturalist movement, but also in a metaphysical sense. His eventual madness, the result of profound suffering, represents the "breakthrough of subterranean forces," not merely an acute case of psychological repression. As in the case of Büchner's *Woyzeck*, Thiel has been "struck a mortal blow, but in such a manner, that the genuine human values still shine brightly in destruction."[18] After the destructive paroxysm has run its course, he lapses into a new humaneness, expressed by his stroking of Tobias's cap. Indeed, even Lene, the "animal" (6:39), is humanized by the mystery of Thiel's suffering. Her sudden softening and reversal of character just before her death is more than the result of fear and remorse; and, although it would be presumptuous to equate it with the kind of "epiphany" Michael Kramer will later experience in the presence of his dead son, there is a tendency in that direction.

More important than content for imbuing the reader with the sense of irrational reality upon which the success of the work depends is the form in which it is presented. Paralleling the admixture of sharp Naturalistic detail and mystical obscurity in the plot is the intermingling of realistic and irrational elements in style and language. The dominant tone of the story, rather pedantically divided into three chapters (atypical for the novella), is that of an objective report interspersed with lyrical passages—the most effective of which depicts Thiel in his forest retreat in communion with his surroundings and

Minna on the eve of the accident (6:48–51). Again, as in *Fasching,* the catastrophe itself is brought into relief in an excited, staccato *Sekundenstil* (6:58) but the subsequent events (with the minor exception of the discovery of the murders) are portrayed in cool, calm tones which tend to neutralize sentimentality. The narrator himself is anonymous but trustworthy. Occasionally he reveals a trace of irony, as when he describes Thiel's ambitions for Tobias who, as his father earnestly hopes, will someday achieve the exalted position of trainmaster (6:43), but Hauptmann avoids outright condescension. On the other hand, he allows the reader to experience the things Thiel experiences; to hear, see, and feel the things that affect him. Empathy with the hero is also facilitated for the educated reader by the lack of dialect, minimal dialogue (for a Naturalistic work), and by Hauptmann's tendency to ascribe to Thiel a sensitivity not normally associated with a character of his social class.

The growing sense of irrationality which precedes the catastrophe and makes it plausible is achieved in various ways; most effectively by a synthesis of two forces usually thought of as opposites: nature and technology. Hauptmann merges the two by describing each in terms of its apparent counterpart, and by imbuing both with the same mystical vitalism that also motivates the characters. Thus, a row of trees is "illuminated as though from within and glows like iron" (6:49); a locomotive stretches its "sinews" (6:60); the moon is described as a "signal lamp" (6:65); the singing telegraph lines become the threatening "web of a giant spider" (6:49); and Lene digs her field "with the speed and endurance of a machine" (6:56). Especially the locomotive, the most impressive representation of the raw power of technology available in 1887, is transformed into a demon of potential destruction. Appearing out of infinity like fate, a dark point on the horizon, suddenly growing into an enormous "black, snorting *Ungetüm*" (i.e., "violence personified" [6:50]), it disappears into unearthly stillness as suddenly and mysteriously as it came—paralleling in its inscrutable origins, sudden destructive force, and equally sudden lapse into deathly calm, Thiel's own fate.

In spite of its Naturalistic exterior a sense of fate pervades the atmosphere of the story. It is enhanced by some of the same techniques Hauptmann had experimented with in *Fasching.* The tragedy is foreshadowed almost from the beginning; ordinary events have symbolic value and their repetition fosters a feeling of inevitability; gesture, silence, and sound are manipulated for maximum effect, as is the virtuoso use of color.

We learn in the very first paragraph, for example, that during the past ten years only two events—both accidents caused by trains—have affected Thiel sufficiently to disrupt his routine and his religious worship. Once he suffered a broken leg when he was struck by a lump of coal falling from a tender, and another time he was struck on the chest by a wine bottle thrown out of an express train racing by him. A few pages later another wine bottle is mentioned, together with a further example of destruction. This time a roebuck has been killed by the Kaiser's special luxury train, and the event is immediately associated with a wine bottle Thiel had found. When he opened it some of the wine gushed forth and he placed it on the shallow edge of a lake only "to lose it somehow or other, so that even years later he still regretted its loss" (6:41).

Both the animal imagery and the symbolic "gushing" appear in meaningful context later. After the death of Tobias another roebuck standing on the fated tracks is spared at the last moment—as though the cravings of a monstrous deity for sacrifice had, for the time being, been satisfied. Likewise, in one of the most vivid scenes of the story— Lene has just been caught abusing Tobias, and Thiel feels an uncontrollable rage—a bottle of milk gushes over and Thiel is suddenly overcome by the sensuality of his wife's swelling breasts and powerful hips. Later Thiel's intuition of the impending accident is aroused by three vertical "milk-white" (6:58) jets of steam which presage the delayed sound of the futile emergency whistle-blasts.

The depiction and juxtaposition of these and similar events is neither coincidental nor gratuitous. They indicate a finely woven fabric of symbolic representation which recapitulates a central theme of the story: the mysterious interrelationship of death and Dionysian vitality.

A similar claim can be made for Hauptmann's use of colors. Sometimes the treatment is so subtle that one can only speculate on its intentionality. Thus, the neutral color brown, which occurs infrequently, links the deer on the tracks with a brown squirrel which Tobias confuses with God,[19] and with Tobias himself through the

emblematic brown *Pudelmützchen* ("little poodle cap") which Thiel
fondles in the asylum at the end of the story. Usually the color
symbolism is more blatant, not to say melodramatic. Dominant by far
are shades of red (representing blood, vitality, etc.) and those associated
with death and decomposition (black, white, etc.). By careful manipulation of the choice of colors, the frequency of their occurrence and even
their intensity (blood-red vs. rose, for example) Hauptmann is able to
foreshadow events, enhance their emotional value, and contribute to
the lyrical unity which has always been the hallmark of the very best
Novellen.

Chapter Three
Anatomy of Family Tragedy

Vor Sonnenaufgang

If Hauptmann had "entered the world as a writer" with *Bahnwärter Thiel*, it was with the play *Vor Sonnenaufgang* [Before Sunrise (1889)] that he made his strongest impact on the history of the German theater and set out on the path that would soon lead him to international fame. He himself later assessed the event more accurately than modestly when he wrote: "Indeed [the play] introduced an original, powerful German literary epoch" (7:1082). A "social drama," according to its subtitle, it represents the author's most extreme concession to the tenets of theoretical Naturalism, almost overwhelming the usual metaphysical wellsprings of his work. To a greater extent than *Thiel* it represents an amalgamation of personal experience, contemporary social opinion, and progressive literary modes. Regarding the latter, Ibsen *(Ghosts, The Wild Duck)* seems not only to have influenced some of the characters, but to have provided as well the basic concept of the "drama of ripe situation" into which a catalyst to the action, in the form of an outsider, is introduced; Zola's "scientific" approach is reflected in Hauptmann's effort to explain the circumstances of a family on economic, hereditary, and environmental grounds; and Tolstoy's *Power of Darkness*—to which the author expressed his special indebtedness—reveals similarities in themes and character relationships as well as in the moral fervor of its attack on corruption.[1]

Closer to home, *Vor Sonnenaufgang* also bears testimony to Hauptmann's indebtedness to Arno Holz. Written in Erkner in 1889 during the early morning summer hours, shortly after his return from Switzerland, it was first published in August of that year with a cordial dedication to "Bjarne P. Holmsen, the most consequent Realist, author of *Papa Hamlet*" (1:10). Holmsen, it turned out, was a pseudonym for the co-authors Holz and Schlaf, and it was Holz who provided the title of Hauptmann's work as well as influencing him in the distinctive

Naturalistic speech patterns of its dialogue.[2] For a brief period Holz was one of the play's most vociferous admirers. In a letter to the author in June, 1889, he praised it as no less than "the best drama that has ever been written in the German language."[3] Holz's admiration was soon cooled by professional jealousy, however, the result of Hauptmann's inordinate success with a Naturalistic style, which Holz felt he himself had created. By the time the play had been performed Hauptmann found it advantageous to dedicate its second edition to two men who could be more useful to him in the future: Otto Brahm and Paul Schlenther, the prime movers of the *Verein Freie Bühne* ("Free Stage Society").[4]

Even before its premiere on the afternoon of October 20, 1889, in Berlin's Lessingtheater, under the auspices of the *Freie Bühne,* the play had aroused so much controversy that a scandal was all but inevitable. On a strictly literary level it intensified the friction between the important rival Naturalist groups in Germany: Michael Georg Conrad's *Gesellschaft* ("Society") circle in Munich and the *Freie Bühne,* dominated by Brahm and Schlenther, in Berlin. Probably still savoring the success of *Thiel,* Hauptmann also submitted *Vor Sonnenaufgang* to *Die Gesellschaft* for publication. There, much to the subsequent chagrin of Conrad and to the detriment of that periodical's continued viability as a leader in the Naturalist movement, it was arbitrarily rejected by co-editor Carl Bleibtreu. Having missed the opportunity to identify itself with the most significant Naturalist work to date, *Die Gesellschaft* bitterly attacked it instead.[5]

In Berlin, where Hauptmann managed to publish the play in book form, it attracted a great deal of attention; very favorable on the part of individuals like Brahm and the renowned and influential novelist and critic Theodor Fontane; very negative from political reactionaries and self-proclaimed protectors of public morality who were as much offended by the socialistic overtones of the drama as by its alleged obscenities.[6] As the premiere date approached, both sides prepared for what was to be the "most momentous theater scandal of German stage history."[7] Amid a pandemonium of boos and cheers the actors (some of whom had received threatening letters) struggled with such distractions as a gynecological forceps waved toward the stage by an agitated medical doctor during the protracted, offstage, birth scene. The sensation created by the twenty-seven-year-old writer was further fueled by the press. Fontane, in what remains one of the best critical appraisals, defended the play calmly and reasonably; the oppositon equated it with bordello literature and condemned its author as the "most immoral playwright of the century."[8]

Seen from a present-day perspective we may wonder what all the fuss was about. Disregarding for the moment the political element, the answer lies in the relativity of moral norms. *Vor Sonnenaufgang* was bound to shock public morality in 1889 because it presented, openly and directly, human degradation to an extent unheard of in previous German belles lettres.

The play describes a type of family that was not uncommon at the time: nouveau riche peasants such as Hauptmann had known personally in Weißstein (the play has Witzdorf) near Salzbrunn, who had come into large fortunes when the coal needed to fuel the Industrial Revolution was discovered under their land. Given the predisposition of the protagonists, the money is more of a curse than a blessing. It allows them to satiate themselves with gourmet foods; keep liveried servants; provide their expensive homes with the latest conveniences such as electric doorbells and telephones, and even to equip their livestock stalls with "marble mangers and silver racks" (1:26). With no externally imposed obligations, they fall easy victim to the sins of the flesh.

The family Hauptmann uses to exemplify this thesis, the Krauses, consists of the owner of the estate, his younger wife, and two daughters from a former marriage: Martha, the older of the two whom we never see, and Helene, twenty-one, the heroine. Hoffmann, an engineer married to Martha, handles the financial affairs of the family and, for reasons which soon become obvious, serves as the head of the household. Gradually, during the course of five acts, the audience is introduced to the full extent of the Krause depravity. The old man spends most of his time in a drunken stupor in the tavern next door and makes crude sexual advances to his daughter, Helene; Mrs. Krause, obviously of low-class background, rather comically attempts to play the grand lady of the manor, while sharing her bed with Wilhelm Kahl, who is both her nephew and Helene's betrothed; Martha, hopelessly addicted to alcohol, is about to have a second child after having lost one son to the ravages of alcohol (at the age of three!), and Hoffmann, an opportunist and sensualist, who, under the guise of solidarity with her, also tries to seduce Helene. Until now, the latter has largely avoided the moral contamination around her (although she has slept with Kahl) by virtue of the fact that she was raised in a pietistic academy for girls and has lived at home for only a short time.

Into this Sodom and Gomorrah Hauptmann introduces his modern Lot—i.e., Loth. Some years earlier Loth and Hoffmann had both been associated with a "Vancouver Island Society." This utopian organization is the fictional equivalent of the "Gesellschaft Pacific," representing a blend of racial and socialist ideals, that had played a role in Hauptmann's own life. In 1884 his friend Alfred Ploetz had actually been sent to America to investigate the so-called "Icarian" settlements in the United States in order to determine the feasibility of founding a similar community under the auspicies of the "Pacific Society." Unfortunately, the conditions he found there were so disheartening that the project was dropped. Unfortunately, too, the society was brought to the attention of governmental authorities and the result was the "Socialist Trial" in 1887 to which Hauptmann was called to testify. Unlike Loth, he was not sent to prison for his activities.[9]

Although he has suffered deprivation, prison, and the loss of a fiancée because of his political activities, Loth's idealistic resolve is as strong as ever. He has come to Witzdorf to investigate and expose the brutal exploitation of the men who work the mines. Since the major local exploiter is none other than Hoffmann, his host, a certain amount of dramatic tension is provoked and, if Hauptmann had continued to stress the conflict between labor and capital, his play would be much more acceptable to present-day socialists. Rather characteristically, he chooses instead to shift the emphasis to a social problem that is politically neutral: hereditary alcoholism.

Again the problem is one with which the author had had intensive personal experience. While still a teen-ager in Breslau, he had developed a dependency on excessive drinking and, later, in Zürich, under the influence of Forel and Ploetz, had been converted for a time into a zealous vegetarian and teetotaler who believed that alcoholism was hereditary.[10] The fact that Loth is a fanatical adherent of these same beliefs precipitates the catastrophe. By the end of the first act it is clear that Helene is deeply attracted to him, and, in the famous, romantic arbor scene of the fourth act, they pledge each other undying devotion. When, in the last act, during a discussion with Martha's attendant physician, Dr. Schimmelpfennig, Loth learns what the audience has known all along—that the Krause family represents a complete contradiction of his vehemently espoused views on hereditary hygiene—he abruptly abandons both his research project and Helene. Simultaneous to his departure, Martha's child is stillborn, and immediately thereafter Helene finds a letter left by Loth and kills herself with a hunting knife.

Reduced to a plot outline in this way, the play seems dated and melodramatic. Its critical stance regarding a specific constellation of problems including alcoholism, political informants, religious hypocrisy, female emancipation, and the rampant chauvinism of German university fraternities—although the problems themselves may still persist—seems quaint and antiquated. And yet, as Fontane recognized, the play has strongly redeeming features which transcend content and find expression in the overall "tone" or atmosphere. "In works of this kind, which have much in common with the ballad," Fontane notes, "the tone is almost everything."[11]

Hauptmann achieves this unifying tone in many different ways. By his own later admission he "wrote *Vor Sonnenaufgang* in such a manner as though the stage didn't have three walls, but four."[12] In spite of any epic tendencies that his play might have, he was not interested in Brechtian "alienation effects." His aim was to involve the spectator emotionally with the people on the stage, to make him forget that he was outside of the action looking in. One much maligned but theatrically effective way of doing this is by creating and maintaining a high level of suspense. The audience is given an almost constant stream of disturbing questions to ponder. What, for example, was the "frightful end" of Hoffmann's son mentioned in the third act? (In Act V we learn that he cut his throat on a bottle he thought contained alcohol.) How will the birth scene be handled when it finally arrives? Will we see Martha? When will Loth, who even in the first act is brought tantalizingly close to the discovery of the Krause family's true nature, have his eyes opened? Will his planned meeting with an earlier friend, Dr. Schimmelpfenning, affect the outcome? What will be the result of the inevitable clash between his ideals and his love of Helene?

On a more subtle level, Hauptmann encourages audience involvement through a number of devices including touches of humor and irony, foreshadowing, effective opening and closing of acts, leitmotif-like repetition, the use of snatches of song familiar to German audiences, pantomime, and a fascinating array of minor characters. The first act opens, for example, with a noisy, theatrically effective dialect scene in which Frau Krause mistakes Loth, who has just arrived for his visit, for a beggar and completely overwhelms and confuses him with the uninhibited vehemence of a crude, peasant outburst (an indication of his ineffectuality in such surroundings), and closes with Helene alone on the stage uttering a fervent prayer: "Oh! don't go, don't go away!" (1:38). For the final act, by contrast, the author specifies that "everything—with few exceptions—is spoken in a subdued tone" (1:82), a direction justified by the drama taking place upstairs in the delivery room. The major exceptions, all the more effective for the quiet which prevails throughout the act, are the hysterical screams of the maid, who discovers Helene's suicide, and the cheerful drunken calling—by now a refrain since we have heard it before—of old Krause: "Ain't I got a coupla pretty daughters?" (1:98) on which the final curtain falls. Similarly effective is the opening scene of Act II (1:39–40)—the predeominantly pantomimic struggle which expresses better than words Helene's desperation in the clutches of her lascivious drunken father—or the last line of Act IV where Kahl, reacting to the commotion aroused by the impending birth of Martha's child, asks with a cynical laugh: "You gonna have a pig slaughter?" (1:81).

To anyone tempted to dismiss Hauptmann's art as crude, Naturalistic sensationalism, his defenders could point to the Romantic love scene in Act IV (1:74–80), in Helene's favorite spot, a small arbor to which she can retreat from her unsavory family. This scene, which is strongly reminiscent of the "Garden" scene of Goethe's *Faust,* is too delicate and musical to be adequately described but some of its elements include Helene's shyly blossoming boldness as she struggles to get Loth to reciprocate her use of the familiar form of the personal pronoun *(du)* with which she addresses him (and which he keeps overlooking); an improvised "litany" of love which she has him repeat after her; her gentle humming of the popular folk melody "Du, du liegst mir im Herzen," (You, you, rest in my heart), and the insinuation of darkly prophetic thoughts about death into the blissful experience of love.

Equally impressive is Hauptmann's skill at characterization. It derives not only from an observant eye and an ear susceptible to the finest linguistic and psychological nuances, but from the fact that many of his best characters are based on people he knew intimately and who often embody traits that he detected in himself. In *Vor Sonnenaufgang* this applies not only to Loth, Hoffmann, and Schimmelpfennig, but also to such minor characters as Hopslabaer and Kahl. The former, an unfortunate, mentally deficient individual with a goiter, goes around selling sand from a child's wagon and provides amusement for local roughnecks by leaping into the air on command. While one would hardly be tempted to equate this character with its author in every detail, Hauptmann's own experiences, such as the traumatic favoritism shown his brother Carl and his cousin Georg, and years of poverty and neglect in Breslau, enabled him to feel more clearly than most what it meant to be a pariah. Even the thoroughly distasteful Kahl seems to reflect personal experience. His stuttering may well be a reflection of Hauptmann's own inarticulateness, and his habit of wandering about shooting small defenseless animals and birds is a weakness the author himself shamefacedly admits to having indulged in as a youth (7:1006–7). The other lesser figures, such as the long-suffering laborer Beibst, the parasitic, hypocritical Frau Spiller (companion to Frau Krause)—even the man who delivers a package—are all three-dimensional characters with their own distinctive language.

More controversial, judging from contemporary and modern criticism, are the "civilized" characters Hoffmann, Schimmelpfennig, Helene, and Loth, perhaps because they are more directly dependent on plot motivation. As individuals they are largely believable. Hoffman, who (like Hauptmann) has married into wealth, is as much weakling as villain, and Schimmelpfennig (like Loth a reflection of the author's experiences with Ploetz and Forel) is a covert idealist who believes that science can be mankind's salavation. Helene[13] is a beautifully conceived young woman with strong emotions and instincts who thinks with her heart as well as her head. Her suicide is abrupt but well motivated by the circumstances and her nature. She has overcome her pride and natural reticence to measure up to Loth's ideas regarding female emancipation (i.e., she has taken the intitiative in their relationship) only to be deserted by her lover for an abstract cause. The fact that she finds his letter moments after having witnessed the death of her alcoholic sister's baby only contributes to her overwrought state of mind. Like Gotthold Ephraim Lessing's Emilia Galotti, her better nature rebels at being drawn ever deeper into the moral morass around her.[14]

The real problem is with Loth. He has been defended, pitied, rejected as a heartless fool, and interpreted as Hauptmann's criticism of his Naturalist cohorts who allowed cold theory to supersede their humanity.[15] By his own admission his strivings have led him to "take on something horribly barren, something machine-like" (1:92), in his nature and, as Schimmelpfennig points out, he is devoid of the saving grace of a sense of humor (1:90). Loth's problems are compounded by those of his creator. By definition, a Naturalist work is a "slice of life," and any attempt to impose a neat, well-rounded ending on it—in harmony with literary tradition—goes counter to the spirit of the movement and to Hauptmann's own predilections. Finally, *Vor Sonnenaufgang,* written with something of the zeal of a political reformer, largely lacks Hauptmann's usual metaphysical orientation, and the ending, an empty sacrifice, is the weaker for it.

Das Friedensfest

Having established a reputation as the latest enfant terrible of German Naturalism with *Vor Sonnenaufgang,* Hauptmann seemed to retreat perceptibly from that movement with his next play, *Das Friedensfest: Eine Familienkatastrophe* [The Coming of Peace: A Family Catastrophe], written in 1889 and published the following year in the *Freie Bühne.* "Critical response" to the new drama "ranged from lukewarm to hostile, and it is only in recent years that it has come to be regarded as a key work in Hauptmann's oeuvre."[16] Even Fontane, to whom it was dedicated, found it inferior to *Vor Sonnenaufgang.* His main reservation was that it was too exclusively concerned with "inner man"—a criticism Hauptmann had foreseen and tried to forestall with a lengthy motto from Lessing.[17] In the meantime, of course, after an intensive schooling in Freud, many modern readers tend to see this alleged defect of the drama as one of its more interesting features. One recent critic even maintains that with *Das Friedensfest* Hauptmann ushered in "the interiorization or psychologizing of the drama."[18]

Like its predecessor, the play is a fascinating mixture of literary and personal experience. An analytical family drama similar to Ibsen's *Ghosts,* it exploits techniques of language and gesture familiar to readers of Büchner and Holz. Much of the plot and some of the character-ization, on the other hand, derive from a personal account by

Frank Wedekind who, incautiously (and much to the detriment of their continued friendship), had confided his family secrets to Hauptmann.[19]

The setting for all three acts is a high-ceilinged living room in a lonely country house near Erkner. The time is Christmas Eve in the 1880s, and the action concerns an unscheduled homecoming of the various members of the strife-torn Scholz family. After a six-year absence, Wilhelm Scholz, a frustrated musician, has allowed himself to be persuaded by Marie Buchner and her daughter Ida, to whom he is emotionally attached, to pay a holiday visit to his mother Minna. His older brother Robert, an author reduced to earning a living by writing advertising slogans, has also returned for his customary yearly visit, and, much to the consternation of the other principals, Dr. Fritz Scholz, the estranged paterfamilias, likewise appears on the scene. Gradually we are introduced to the "case history" of a family. Always tenuous at best, the cohesion of the group had finally dissolved six years ago. Enraged over what he considered insulting behavior toward his mother, Wilhelm had struck his father full in the face. This impetuous act not only precipitated his own and his father's departure, but estranged him from the other members of the family as well.

Years of guilt and regret, the humanizing influence on Wilhelm of the Buchner women, and perhaps the festive atmosphere of the Christmas season have now prepared the ground for a reconciliation. In the middle of the second act, the center of the play, the miracle occurs. Wilhelm has just confessed the details of his transgression against his father to Ida when the old man appears on the staircase—descending from his upstairs apartment, where he had previously lived separated from his family and to which he had immediately fled upon his return. Upon seeing him, Wilhelm's usual articulateness deserts him and in a pantomimic scene of great intensity he stammers out his guilt, receives his father's absolution, and falls into a deathlike unconsciousness from which he is revived fresh and relaxed—a new man with the potential for creative achievement. For a short time a happy ending appears likely; even the cynical Robert seems to fall under the spell of the new harmony. Unfortunately, the emotional chemistry between the various protagonists seems to preclude anything more than sporadic sputterings of affection. Bickering, mostly instigated by Robert over seemingly inconsequential incidents, sets in once more, and by the end of the act the old animosities are stronger than ever.

The last act takes place in subdued light, provided by the semi-extinguished chandelier and a single candle left burning on the Christmas tree. The mood is equally dark. Recrimination follows recrimination. Wilhelm reverts to new depths of despair and is about to accept Robert's argument that, in analogy to the marriage of his parents, he and Ida have no chance for happiness, when the final bombshell falls: the father, whose health has been precarious, suddenly dies. The curtain falls on an ambiguous scene. Wilhelm, barely mastering his pain and seething emotions, takes Ida's hand in his and "goes, . . . upright and composed toward the next room" (1:165) where his father lies dead.

Again a mere plot outline—which excludes such interesting minor characters as Dr. Scholz's servant Friebe and his daughter Auguste—provides very little insight into the complexity of the drama. Hauptmann's most succinct statement of a favorite idea, i.e., "what one gives to the action, one takes from the characters" (6:1043), suggests a more productive point of departure. Here, to a greater extent than in *Vor Sonnenaufgang,* the characters not only verbalize the ideas of their creator, but embody them in their personalities. Naturalist crassness is replaced by psychological nuance. The one "shocking" event, Wilhelm's striking of his father, occurred six years before the scenes we are allowed to observe. What we experience are the ramifications of an act rather than the act itself. And, although *Das Friedensfest* is considerably shorter than its five-act predecessor, its structural compactness permits the treatment, in greater depth, of a wider range of problems.

Since an author's favorite ideas tend to reflect the cultural ambience of his era, his upbringing, and his personal preoccupations, we should not be surprised to find a certain overlapping of themes from work to work. While the emphasis and treatment differs, this is true for *Vor Sonnenaufgang* and *Das Friedensfest.* Both works touch upon problems such as that of the "marriage lie"; the analysis of family life; nouveau riche peasants (the Krause family and Minna Scholz); the determinism of heredity; the influence of a changed environment (Helene's upbringing in a private school and the influence of the Buchner household on Wilhelm); and the dangers of alcohol. Whereas *Vor Sonnenaufgang* stresses more overtly the problems of female emancipation and contemporary politics, *Das Friedensfest* opens discussions on pedagogy, the generation gap, and the problems of being an artist.

Occasionally a topic treated in the earlier play is hardly recognizable in the latter. A case in point is alcohol. In *Vor Sonnenaufgang* a hereditary predisposition to drink is central to both the action and the atmosphere of the play; in *Das Friedensfest* it is very easily overlooked although, quite conceivably, it too contributes to the outcome of the "family catastrophe." And, while it would be an exaggeration to ascribe the final clash between Robert, his father, and Wilhelm to alcohol alone, its excessive consumption by two of the principals may well have exacerbated the vehemence of Robert's outbursts vis-à-vis Ida and Wilhelm and contributed to the intensity of the persecution mania that seizes Dr. Scholz the last time we see him alive. That this aspect of the play has been so consistently overlooked is a tribute to Hauptmann's subtle artistry. Instead of being faced with a Naturalistic depiction of drunken revelry (in the manner of old Krause) we are dependent on sporadic stage directions and casual comments to provide clues to what is happening offstage. For example, shortly after the arrival of Dr. Scholz and his exit to the upstairs apartment, his faithful confidant and servant Friebe is seen leaving the cellar "carrying, in his left hand, three bottles of red wine . . . in such a manner that the necks are clamped between his fingers—, under his left armpit a bottle of cognac" (1:118). Later Friebe, who is almost constantly alone with the old man, is depicted as quite patently drunk (1:141–42) and Dr. Scholz himself appears with "drink-reddened face" (1:143). That Robert, too, has been imbibing too freely is suggested by his mother's concern: "If only Robert didn't drink so much." Wilhelm naively assures her: "Oh, mother, today . . . today all that makes no difference!" (1:141).

Another factor that militates against a peaceful denouement, is the enmity of the two brothers, specifically Robert's jealous envy of Wilhelm's relationship to Ida. Again the subject is treated subtly and with a strong reliance on precise stage directions. In the first act, for example, Robert is left alone on the stage when he notices a purse Ida had crocheted for her deceased father and brought as a Christmas present for Wilhelm: "Looking about nervously like a thief, he bends down again, hastily seizes the yellow silk purse, brings it closer to his eyes and, with a sudden passionate movement, to his lips. This moment shows the flash of an uncanny, pathological ardor" (1:123). Later, when Ida presents her gift to Wilhelm, Robert ridicules it (1:143) and, by his uncouth behavior, turns the festive occasion into one of acrimony. Under these circumstances Wilhelm's accusation that his brother envies him Ida's love (1:163) is eminently plausible.

While alcohol and jealousy provide tinder for the conflagration, a more basic theme is the question of fate (overtly expressed as the determinism of heredity and environment) versus human willpower. Working in the strong contrasts so typical of Naturalist drama, Hauptmann devises an experiment in which the forces of optimism and love, embodied in Marie and Ida Buchner, clash with the pessimism and equally human, though less attractive, attributes of Minna and Robert Scholz—with the vacillating and neurasthenic Wilhelm somewhere in the middle. When Mrs. Buchner first arrives on the scene, she is convinced that a little love, understanding, and sincere effort is all that is needed for reconciliation and harmony. Her seemingly less intelligent, and certainly less appealing, counterpart, Mrs. Scholz, is much more skeptical of the efficacy of willing things to happen (Cf. 1:112). During the first half of the play it appears that Mrs. Buchner's attitude has been vindicated, but the vehemence of the relapse into family discord opens her eyes. Her faith in willpower is badly shaken and she confesses to Wilhelm: "I came here with a firm, cheerful faith. I'm downright ashamed. What did I take on! I wanted to influence such personalities, I a weak, simple, person!—Now everything is reeling. I suddenly feel my frightful responsibility . . ." (1:155).

If Mrs. Buchner has to be educated to skepticism, Robert Scholz seems to be a freewheeling cynic from the start. In his view, the family is hopelessly burdened by the mistakes of the parents: "A man of forty marries a girl of sixteen and drags her into this godforsaken corner. A man who served as a physician in Turkey and traveled in Japan. A cultivated, enterprising spirit. A man who was still preoccupied with the most far-reaching plans gets together with a woman who, until a few years ago, was completely convinced that one could see America as a star in the heavens. Really! I'm not fooling. Well, and it turned out accordingly: a stagnant, rotten, fermenting swamp from which we have the dubious pleasure of originating. Hair-raising! Love—not a trace. Mutual understanding—don't ask; and this is the [flower] bed upon which we children grew" (1:120).

Here Hauptmann reflects the prevalent view of his day that a marriage entered into for financial reasons rather than love produces defective progeny. For the Scholz family the problem is compounded by faulty education and training. As Robert summarizes, the children "are all thoroughly botched. Botched in origin; completely botched in upbringing" (1:121).

What this upbringing was like we hear from Wilhelm. While he admits that his father's intentions may have been good, he insists that the results were disastrous. Vacillating between periods of brutal authoritarianism and equally callous neglect, Dr. Scholz seems to have been as much concerned with triumphing over the influence of his wife as with his sons' welfare (Cf. 1:131–32). On this background both Robert and Wilhelm place much of the blame for their failure in life.

Here, then, is the confrontation of two conflicting views: the initial Buchner optimism and belief that man has a measure of control over his destiny and the more pessimistic view, embodied in the experience of the Scholz family, that we are the victims of circumstances. While both sides have moments of apparent triumph, neither is decisively victorious. True, upon learning of the death of his father at the end of the play, Wilhelm rallies from his deepest pessimism, takes Ida's hand, and appears to march resolutely into the future. The very suddenness of his change in attitude, however, casts deep suspicions on its permanence, and we are not at all convinced that the young couple has been freed from the toils of the past. Hauptmann's personal views contribute little in the way of clarification. "Optimism as such," he wrote, "has something suspicious about it, more: something vulgar, more: something banal, more: something vile!—But pessimism too gives the impression of something shopworn and is in every sense an appropriate contrast to the above: for concepts are totally inadequate when it is a matter of even so much as touching upon the mystery of existence" (6:998).

Remarks such as this should caution us against a simplistic interpretation of the play as a kind of literary demonstration of the laws of heredity and environment. Indeed, if there were no more to it than that, one could agree with Eberhard Hilscher that it can no longer claim more than historical interest.[20] Considering, however, Hauptmann's lifelong belief in the ultimate ineffability of human existence, the preponderant evidence of his work, and the clues provided by *Das Friedensfest* itself, Karl S. Guthke seems closer to the mark when he postulates a *Tiefenschicht,* a deeper level, to the play in which man represents considerably more than the sum of his heredity and environment.[21] From this perspective, such deterministic forces are merely agents of a more profound fate which proscribes human behavior. For *Das Friedensfest,* with its archetypal conflict between father and son over the mother, or the bitter enmity between brothers, such an interpretation is especially attractive.[22] And, since the type of conflicts described predate articulated concepts and tend to express themselves in gestures and actions rather than words, it is both appropriate and significant that Hauptmann chose to represent their (temporary) resolution in a pantomimic scene culminating in the unconsciousness of his hero. In a process familiar to readers of Goethe's *Iphigenie,* Kleist's *Prinz Friedrich von Homburg,* and numerous works by Hauptmann himself, catharsis follows emotional suffering too great to bear. There is a lapse into a substratum of authentic existence, a state of lucid unconsciousness, in which the inescapable antinomies of good and evil, innocence and guilt are miraculously reconciled and from which the sufferer emerges with that "peace which passeth all understanding." This is what happens to Wilhelm, and it is a testimonial to the validity of his experience that those who witness it are themselves affected—albeit only temporarily since it is in the very nature of such "epiphanies" that they remain ephemeral.

Considering the verisimilitude of psychological nuance and intimately conceived characters (each carefully delineated as to appearance, speech rhythm, and quirks of behavior) it seems unlikely that Hauptmann's play is only the thinly disguised depiction of problems encountered in Frank Wedekind's family. More plausibly, he used Wedekind's revelations as the basis for his minimal plot but enriched them with experiences from his own life. Thus Wedekind had, to be sure, supplied the background of his parents' marriage and the story of how he himself had struck his father over an insult to his mother and had subsequently been forced to leave home and prostitute his writing talent in the service of advertising before a reconciliation was finally brought about. He seems not, however, to have had anything to do with the characters of Auguste, of Marie Buchner, or of her daughter Ida (and thus with the considerable romantic interest of the plot) nor with the prominent theme of enmity between brothers. Furthermore, the models for characters he did provide—especially his father, his mother, and himself—are not identical with their fictional counterparts. And while

Wilhelm-Robert may be an analysis of Wedekind's own character into its idealistic and cynical components, it also seems likely that the two characters owe something to the play's author and his brother Carl. Certainly there is ample biographical evidence to link the generally competitive and combative realtionship of the Hauptmann brothers to Robert and Wilhelm.[23] And while there is no need to go so far as to simply *identify* Robert with Carl Hauptmann on the basis of personality traits, Frederick W. J. Heuser's observation that some of Robert's tirades were taken almost verbatim from a letter written by Carl[24] at least suggests an affinity between the two in the author's mind.

A similar relationship between Hauptmann's sister Johanna and his mother Marie, on the one hand, and the Scholz women—Auguste and Minna—on the other would also seem to be a distinct possibility. Except that the age difference between Auguste and Wilhelm has been halved from six to three years (as has been that of Robert and Wilhelm from four to two), Auguste seems to be, physically and psychologically, a rather accurate portrait of Johanna.[25] More striking still are the similarities between Marie Hauptmann and Minna (again a diminutive form of the name Marie) Scholz, perhaps because of the much more central role she has in the play. Not only is the conflict between father and mother a frequent theme in Hauptmann's work but the portrait of Minna Scholz seems much closer to that of his own mother than that of Frau Wedekind. Mésalliances, to be sure, figure prominently in both families. In the Wedekind household, however, the father was a well-travelled medical doctor and the mother was a highly gifted singer and actress—in addition to being the daughter of a rich factory owner.[26]

Frau Scholz lacks completely even the minimal sophistication one would associate with such a background. As was the case in the Hauptmann family, her interests are of a banal commercial nature (e.g., is Ida sufficiently wealthy to justify her son's interest in her? [Cf. 1:153]). Without a trace of intellectual or cultural ambition, her idea of a wife's obligations are equated with keeping her husband supplied with warm socks (1:150), completely ignoring any claim he might have to a deeper, more spiritual companionship. Seemingly blind to such values, she complains constantly and bitterly about the father to her children, not hesitating even to stoop to the moral blackmail of melodramatically beseeching God to rescue her from this vale of tears

(1:147). This is very similar to the image of Marie Hauptmann and her relationship to her husband and children that we get from her son's autobiographical writings.[27]

The purpose of such remarks about the biographical nature of *Das Friedensfest* is not to sort out the various factual strands which are reflected in the work, or even to diminish the importance of the Wedekind influence. The play is too homogeneous to permit such roughshod analysis, and Wedekind's incautious confessions do seem to have provided Hauptmann with its initial impetus—while at the same time distracting his readers from too close a scrutiny of its more private elements. The investigation of such biographical material has a different justification: it reveals a personal involvement that helps us to comprehend better the emotional intensity of its author's creative investment.

Einsame Menschen

The next drama, *Einsame Menschen* [Lonely Lives] was written in 1889 and first performed in 1890. Like its predecessors, it takes up the problems of an idealist in conflict with a family enmeshed in mistakes of the past and incapable of understanding his more progressive aspirations. Again there is a similar constellation and typology of characters: an older and a younger couple; a cynical counterpart to the idealistic hero; and an outsider whose sudden appearance disturbs the precarious balance of the troubled family.

The scene is Friedrichshagen—for Hauptmann and his young friends as much a state of mind as a place,[28] and the play opens with the offstage sounds of a baptismal ceremony. Although he no longer believes in the ritual, Johannes Vockerat has allowed his infant son to be baptized to satisfy his fundamentalist parents. A former student of theology, the young father now decorates the walls of his living room with portraits of Charles Darwin and the materialist philosopher Ernst Haeckel, and is at work on a bio-philosophical magnum opus which even his artist friend, the outwardly cynical Braun, finds more than a bit ludicrous. Egotistically obsessed with his work—the more so since he is counting on it to vindicate a seemingly botched existence— Johannes has increasingly alienated himself from those around him. His wife Käthe, an uneducated but sincere young woman reared in the ideals of "children, church, and kitchen" typical of her generation, suffers most. She feels totally inadequate and unable to provide her husband with the understanding and support she feels is expected of her.

Into this tense emotional situation, already exacerbated by the tensions of parenthood, Hauptmann introduces "the other woman," Anna Mahr, one of those rare female students then beginning to appear on the university scene. Although not especially attractive physically, she seems to be everything Käthe is not: exotic, liberated, strong, and an intellectual match for Johannes. She has dropped by to see her old friend Braun on her way back to her sociological studies at the University of Zürich, but she and Johannes are immediately attracted to each other and she is easily persuaded to remain for a few days as a house guest. As their relationship intensifies into something suspiciously similar to love, the marriage deteriorates. The parents warn their son that his behavior is tantamount to adultery of the heart and, after several attempts supported by Braun, persuade Anna to leave, in spite of Johannes's passionately proclaimed conviction that their relationship represents a new ideal communion between man and woman. The play ends abruptly with Käthe's collapse upon discovering a note left behind when Johannes impulsively fled the house. Outside we hear Braun calling out for him in the direction of the lake. While not specifically mentioned, suicide is a distinct possibility.

Half a century after its appearance Hauptmann still expressed a special fondness for *Einsame Menschen,* and sensitive contemporaries (e.g., Anton Chekhov) were deeply moved by it.[29] Recent criticism tends to be less enthusiastic. In spite of its obvious virtues—especially the author's skill in evoking atmosphere and in suggesting delicate psychological nuances—modern audiences find it melodramatic and even inadvertently humorous, probably because it is difficult to sympathize with either its hero or his naive views. Whatever its flaws, the drama is an important document for understanding the mood and ideas of the young author and his generation.

To an even greater degree than *Das Friedensfest, Einsame Menschen* has stimulated literary and biographical detective work. Of its various literary ancestors, the most significant is Ibsen's *Rosmersholm* (1887). In that analytical "drama of ripe situation," impelled toward tragedy by the intrusion of a scheming woman, we encounter a number of motifs and character types that reappear three years later in Hauptmann's play. For example, Johannes Rosmer, his recently deceased wife Beate, and Rebecca West have much in common with Johannes Vockerat, Käthe, and Anna Mahr. Like his counterpart Rosmer, Vockerat has abandoned a career as a pastor and become something of a freethinker and, like Rosmer and Rebecca West, he and Anna Mahr are preoccupied with the idea of a spiritualized "marriage" based on friendship rather than sex.[30]

Such parallels notwithstanding, *Einsame Menschen* is, of course, much more than a *Rosmersholm redivivus*. Tentatively titled *Martin und Martha* and *Das Wunderkind* [The Prodigy], the play is dedicated "to those who lived it." Hauptmann later explained that he had in mind an episode from his brother Carl's life involving a marital crisis with his wife Martha over Josefa Krzyzanowska, a Polish student studying in Zürich.[31] Indeed, there are strong similarities between the principals of this episode and those of the play. Like Johannes, Carl was an almost pathologically irritable and impatient idealist at work on an ambitious book on *Metaphysik in der modernen Physiologie* (the first part of which was published in 1893), and like Anna Mahr, Josefa "understood" him and encouraged him in his work. Beyond this, however, and in spite of a decided physical resemblance betweeen Carl and Johannes Vockerat, the parallels are more difficult to pinpoint. It soon becomes obvious that the characters are composites of traits from different models and that, in their final form, they transcend any and all of these models and assume a life of their own. Thus, Käthe is an amalgamation of Martha and Marie Hauptmann (although neither of these women was as simple or weak as her fictional counterpart), and the elder Frau Vockerat appears to be something of a hybrid of the author's own mother and his pietistic aunt Julie Schubert.

The most interesting of these composites is Johannes himself. Although he embodies some of Carl's characteristics, and lives in Friedrichshagen (as did Carl), a number of events described in the play relate more directly to Gerhart than to his brother. It was Gerhart, for example, who strongly resisted the baptism of his son; it was he whom his mother visited in order to assist with the birth of the child, and it is in relation to himself that he brings up the motif of his mother's dissatisfaction over his career. Furthermore, Johannes is twenty-eight years old—the same age as Hauptmann when he wrote the play—and shares with him a number of other traits such as his chest pains.[32]

An increased awareness of Hauptmann's identification with his hero suggests that *Einsame Menschen* was created in much the same manner as *Das Friedensfest*. In the latter Wedekind's experiences provided the author with a façade which could conceal the origins of his own, more intimate confessions; here brother Carl's story serves that function. As in the case of Goethe's *Werther* (with whom, incidentally, the frustrated musician Wilhelm Scholz and the frustrated writer Johannes Vockerat have much in common),[33] the fate of a real person becomes a vehicle for poetic self-expression.

In order for an author to use such borrowed experience effectively it must deeply concern him. For *Das Friedensfest* it was Hauptmann's own strong feelings about family life and the rivalry between brothers that provided the necessary fascination; for *Einsame Menschen* it seems to have been his marriage.

Although it is unlikely that there was a single, real-life equivalent of Anna Mahr to intrude upon his own marriage while he was writing the play, his relationship with Marie was already strained and he had come perilously close to infidelity. In *Das Abenteuer meiner Jugend* he describes an idyllic episode he had experienced in Capri with Malja Brückner, the plain but intellectually brilliant daughter of a German professor. While Carl argued philosophy with the father, Gerhart was delightfully absorbed in discussions of utopias, about which she was very knowledgeable with Malja. Had she remained even a week longer in Capri, he admits, he would "at the very least, have had a burden of conscience to bear in regard to Mary, even if we had had the strength to avoid the most extreme conflict."[34]

Perhaps it is also not too farfetched to see *Einsame Menschen* itself as a kind of experiment in infidelity on Hauptmann's part, since it represents a rather remarkable foreshadowing of the dissolution of his own marriage a few years later.

While *Einsame Menschen* contributes to a deeper understanding of its author's personality and creative approach, its greater significance lies in the fact that its hero is paradigmatic for the general zeitgeist to be found among a certain segment of the younger generation in Germany around 1890. Johannes is an *Ubergangsmensch* ("transitional man") who, while proclaiming his new ideals of personal morality, women's rights, and natural religion, is, in reality, stuck between a past he professes to despise and a future he is too weak to grasp. Whereas his parents are still very much at home in their world and secure in the innocence of their convictions, he is an outsider, no longer supported either by the religious certainty of his parents, or by the optimistic nineteenth-century faith in science and social progress. Like the young men of the Friedrichshagen group with whom Hauptmann frequently met, Johannes's speculations are more personal and ethical than universal and scientific in nature: problems dealing with the "new morality," changing relationships between the sexes, free love, friendship, and related subjects, which by this time had also come to dominate the pages of the *Freie Bühne.*

While the play contains a certain amount of criticism of the status quo (obligatory for a Naturalist work), neither Hauptmann, Johannes, nor, for that matter, the majority of the German Naturalists were social revolutionaries.[35] The difference between the older generation and the younger lies, rather, in the degree of awareness of the problems of their age than in an energetic program for their solution. Thus, Martha Vockerat, the orthodox Christian, comfortably salves her conscience by offering kitchen scraps to the poor washerwoman Frau Lehmann (1:186), and Johannes, much like Loth in *Vor Sonnenaufgang,* is so egocentric that he exhausts his moral fervor in speculation rather than deeds. In theory he is against the rite of baptism; for a redistribution of material wealth (he once considered giving everything away and living in poverty); for female emancipation, and for a sexually desensitized relationship between men and women. In practice he allows his son to be baptized; squanders his and his wife's money while ignoring the poor around him; treats Käthe as an inferior; succumbs to physical love in his platonic relationship (as evidenced by the "long, fervent kiss" [1:245] with which he and Anna separate), and, finally, submits to the pressure of contemporary mores. Even his "suicide," since it is suggested rather than stated, has an air of vacillation about it, and one leaves the play unconvinced that Johannes is any better than his parents—at least theirs is a *blind* hypocrisy.

Although less blatantly so, Johannes, like his parents, is still a product of the past and, at best, as Braun sums him up, "a compromiser" (1:203). The country house he chooses to live in symbolizes his retreat from the real problems of the modern metropolis; his living room is decorated with pictures of Darwin and Haeckel side by side with popular religious paintings; the book he is writing is neither science nor philosophy but a combination of both, and, in spite of his progressive views, the language and pathos with which he expresses them shows him to be a belated Romantic.[36]

The fact that Johannes from today's perspective is also something of a bore is, however, not sufficient reason to reject the entire play out of hand. Hauptmann's craftsmanship, characterization, and depiction of subsurface psychological nuances (in the relationship between Braun and Anna, for example) are of a high order; as are his treatment of time and his virtuoso manipulation of literary allusions, snatches of folk songs, or biblical quotations to enhance the "autumnal glow"[37] of the play's delicate fin-de-siècle atmosphere.

Chapter Four
Blessed are the Poor
Die Weber

First published in the dialect of the Eulengebirge region of Silesia in 1892, *De Waber* was transformed by Hauptmann during the spring of the same year into a much more widely accessible dialect-flavored High-German version: *Die Weber: Schauspiel aus den vierziger Jahren* [The Weavers: A Play from the Forties]. This work, and especially the political turmoil provoked by its staging, were to thrust its thirty-year-old author into the arena of world opinion in a way that the relatively local scandal of *Vor Sonnenaufgang* had failed to do.

In the years since its appearance *Die Weber* has been acclaimed as "that work of young Hauptmann in which his human as well as his literary qualities speak out most strongly and clearly" as the first (revolutionary) "drama of the masses" in German literature, and quite simply as "the greatest Naturalist drama."[1] In a panegyric not at all atypical Hugh F. Garten characterizes it as "the supreme achievement of Naturalistic drama, at the same time transcending all aesthetic theories by its dramatic power and emotional impact."[2]

The political impact of *Die Weber* particularly was such that it brought Hauptmann almost instant renown and/or notoriety (a distinction frequently dependent on the political orientation of the critic or observer) and contributed strongly to a distortion of his image which can still be felt today. Even before the completion of the non-dialect version—as early as February 20, 1892—the play had become the subject of "the most spectacular political censorship trial in the history of German literature."[3] On the right end of the political spectrum the tendency was to see this ostensibly historical play as a thinly disguised attack on contemporary social conditions; worse still, as a dangerous incitement to revolution. For leftists, then and more recently, it aroused more ambivalent feelings. Depending partly on the manner in which it was performed, it could be seen as a fanfare of protest against capitalist oppression. As such, it was translated into Russian by Lenin's sister and had an impact not only on Russian literature but on the Russian Revolution itself.[4] For many of the more thoughtful Marxist critics, however, the play remained a disappointment. While the first four acts seemed to legitimize Hauptmann as one of their own, the quietism of Act V soon became a source of puzzlement and serious concern.

The first act of *Die Weber* takes place in a large, desolate shipping room in Wilhelm Dreissiger's house in Peterswaldau where the weavers of the region—easily recognized by their uniformly emaciated and poverty-stricken appearance—have assembled to deliver piecework woven in their homes, and to plead for a little extra money to keep from starving. Pfeifer, himself a former weaver now working for Dreissiger, serves as his employer's intermediary with the weavers and seems to derive sadistic pleasure from ridiculing them, steadfastly refusing their pleas, and trying to lower even further their already ridiculous wages.

A first flickering confrontation between prosperous and poor occurs with the appearance of Bäcker, a young and atypically vigorous weaver. Unlike the others, he refuses to be humiliated, speaks out boldly, and demands his rights. Pfeifer, unable to handle the situation himself, calls in the corpulent, asthmatic Dreissiger. In the ensuing argument we learn that Bäcker is one of a group of militant weavers from Bielau who have been annoying the factory owner and his family by marching past their window singing the infamous *Blutgericht* ("Court of Blood" and/or "Bloody Revenge"), the rallying song of the oppressed textile workers. Still refusing to be intimidated, Bäcker is every bit a match for his opponent, and the dangerous situation is only defused by a chance incident which attracts everyone's attention: an eight-year-old boy, sent on behalf of his family, collapses from hunger and is removed to Dreissiger's office. Dreissiger seizes the opportunity to expound hypocritically on the irresponsibility of the weavers, the burdens of his position, and the harassment he and his fellow businessmen suffer from the press. The act closes with a dubious concession. Dreissiger expresses his willingness to employ two hundred additional weavers, fully aware, of course, that this will depress the general wage scale even more.

Having introduced his collective hero—the masses of suffering weavers—in the first act, Hauptmann gives us a microscopic view of a typical family, in the second. As the curtain rises, old Robert Baumert's wife, daughters, idiot son, and ragged, four-year-old grandson, are anxiously awaiting his arrival home. The fear that he may be squandering desperately needed food money in a tavern proves unfounded when he arrives in the company of Moritz Jäger, a recently discharged soldier. Aided by Jäger's more positive outlook, a bottle of liquor, and the rare prospect of meat for dinner—the Baumerts have slaughtered the family dog—the mood seems almost bright. Unfortunately, the rich, unaccustomed fare proves too much for Baumert and his stomach rejects it. Deeply moved by this most palpable sign of human degradation, Jäger reads aloud from the inflammatory *Blutgericht* and manages to excite even the old man to rebellious expressions of hatred.

By shifting the scene of Act III to a local tavern Hauptmann is able to introduce yet another set of characters and viewpoints, provide occasional touches of comic relief, and comment unobtrusively on the roles played by the government, business, police, and social hierarchy in the weavers' plight. In rapid succession, a traveling salesman displays his ignorance of local conditions and is pushed aside; a group of young rebels, led by Bäcker and Jäger, are incited by the remarks of the blacksmith Wittig to begin singing their forbidden song; efforts by Kutsche, the local policeman, to prevent them prove totally ineffectual, and the singers end by taking their song of protest openly into the streets.

Set in the cold, elegant comfort of Dreissiger's private home, Act IV provides another strong contrast. The opening confrontation involves Weinhold, a pale, thin nineteen-year-old youth with long blond hair, who is both a theology student and the tutor of Dreissiger's children; Pastor Kittelhaus, a cheerful, morally insenstive, and ineffectual friend of the house; and Dreissiger himself. Through the interaction of these characters and within the space of a few pages, Hauptmann manages to offer a scathing indictment of the collusion of church and capital so typical of the contemporary situation: by hesitatingly broaching the opinion that their extreme privation might have something to do with the dissatisfaction of the weavers—expressed once more by the sound of their familiar song from outside—Weinhold shocks the older minister and provokes his own, on-the-spot dismissal by Dreissiger. Meanwhile the rebels march on the house. Jäger, by now an acknowledged ringleader, is arrested by Dreissiger's men and brought inside for interrogation by police supervisor Heide. When the threat from outside continues to grow, Heide foolishly attempts to remove him to safer custody but is beaten by the mob and relieved of his prisoner. Dreissiger, his family, and the despised factotum Pfeifer barely manage to escape, and when the intruders find the house empty they set about demolishing everything in sight.

After the commotion at the end of Act IV the final act opens quietly, in the subdued morning light of a weaver's dismal home, with a prayer. Old Hilse, fully at ease in his patriarchal role, in spite of his ravaged body, presides over his family (including his blind, almost deaf wife, his son Gottlieb, his daughter-in-law Luise, and his pretty, seven-year-old granddaughter Mielchen) and the start of a new work day. Unlike the members of the younger generation, the old man leads an existence devoid of mortal anxieties and grounded in a pietistic religiosity which makes the materialistic problems of the present pale into insignificance compared with the eternal bliss of the life to come. Even here, however, the world begins to intrude: first by the arrival of the ragpicker Hornig, who brings news of the struggle being waged outside, and, more directly, by Mielchen, who brings her mother a silver spoon she has found among the rubble, with the shy request that she get a dress with the money it will yield. Hilse, however, and (to an only slightly lesser degree) Gottlieb are horrified by the "theft" and make immediate plans for the restitution of the object to its owner. Only Luise questions the deeper morality of such a move and points out that this relatively insignificant piece of private property could provide the family with many weeks of sustenance. This small incident signals the collapsing solidarity of the family. When the rebels call their comrades out into the street, first Luise and eventually Gottlieb join in their fanatical rage. Old Hilse, who remains behind seated at his loom, the place assigned him by his "heavenly Father," dies there—a victim of a stray bullet whistling through his window.

Seen in the context of Hauptmann's work and of the contemporary literary situation, *Die Weber* was indeed a unique contribution. For its author it represented a first application of Naturalist theory and technique to documented, historical subject matter; and for the German stage it was a major step away from the traditional "classical" or

"closed" form of drama to a more "open," indeed "epic," form. As a
Naturalist play it epitomizes the favorite ideas and techniques of the
movement. The inherent determinism of milieu is all-pervasive—to
the extent that the weavers' very bodies have been deformed by endless
labor in cramped postures behind their looms. On the one hand, the
sheer uniformity of their lot—constant hunger, inadequate light and
lack of sunshine, dusty working conditions, the necessity of constant
work by all members of the family to keep from starving—imposes a
terrible sameness of appearance and outlook on Hauptmann's workers.
On the other hand, through extensive, careful stage directions and an
almost microscopic attention to detail—especially linguistic detail—
the author manages to imbue all but the most peripheral of his
characters with unique personalities. Each speaks in his own characteristic language with distinctive dialectal inflections, idiomatic
peculiarities, syntax, speech rhythm and melody, and even gestures.
The result is a portrait of the masses that differs radically from similar
efforts which preceded and were soon to follow it. In contrast to Georg
Büchner's *Dantons Tod* or Christian Dietrich Grabbe's *Napoleon oder die
hundert Tage* with which it is sometimes compared, Hauptmann ele-
vates his masses from the status of stage extras, designed to enhance the
atmosphere of revolution, to a central role, the "collective hero."[5] By
avoiding the tendency toward an abstract portrayal of the masses (so
typical of German Expressionist drama), by individualizing and
humanizing his weavers, he likewise assures a heavy emotional investment in their plight on the part of his audience. Unlike Brecht, who, at
least in theory, aimed at liberating the intellect in the service of a
specific program, Hauptmann remained content to arouse deeply felt
human compassion. That this strategy sometimes, as in the episode of
little Mielchen and the silver spoon, could lead him dangerously close
to sentimentality, was a risk his superb artistry permitted him to take.

   In a very real (albeit non-Brechtian) sense *Die Weber* has strongly epic
tendencies; a fact which has aroused the consternation especially of
those critics who have approached it with preconceived notions as to
what a well-made drama should be.[6] Restricted by historical facts and a
large dramatis personae from producing the traditional pyramid-
structure of logical, step-by-step exposition with a climax inevitably
reached in the third of five acts, and with the conflict evolving from the
clash of a few strong protagonists, Hauptmann chose a more flexible

approach: a series of thematically related, loosely connected tableaux in the manner of Büchner's *Woyzeck*. Such a change—basically the switch from an architectonic to a musical design—must be judged on its own intrinsic merits. In *Die Weber* Hauptmann succeeds in producing a sense of unity and totality appropriate to a Naturalist drama; i.e., to a drama incapable of veering too obviously from the facts of the particular "slice of life" that its author is trying to represent.

This unity is achieved in various subtle ways: old Robert Baumert appears in all five acts (as does at least one of the fanatical revolutionaries, Jäger or Bäcker); Act V represents a recapitulation in miniature of the rising tide of revolt; and the song of the *Blutgericht* traces, from its first halting and subdued introduction in Act I to its use as the noisy public battle cry of the later acts, the spreading crescendo of violent open rebellion. As Hans Rabl demonstrates in his somewhat simplistic but still cogent study,[7] the acts themselves are also carefully orchestrated for maximum emotional impact. Reduced to schematic form, they represent a veritable fever chart of the revolt. Thus the second, third, and fourth act each begins at a higher emotional pitch than its predecessor and ends higher still. Act V, on the other hand, in keeping with its function as a recapitulation, begins somewhat lower on the scale but then rises higher than all the others.[8] In the final analysis, of course, the deeper unity of the play is centered in the suffering of the weavers themselves.

The novelty of its formal, artistic innovations notwithstanding, it is problems of content—especially the relationship of Act V and the character of Hilse to the rest of the drama—that have fueled the controversy over *Die Weber*. The play's early reception has been thoroughly documented elsewhere,[9] and the furor attending it can only be explained on the basis of the German political situation during the latter part of the nineteenth century and the ambiguity of its message. Although Hauptmann's ultimate intentions and the degree of his political sophistication will probably remain open to debate, it soon became obvious that he had touched a raw nerve of the body politic. At a time when socialist ideas were rapidly spreading (due, to a large extent, to the problems of Germany's belated industrialization) and when these ideas were being obsessively opposed by a repressive regime, a bourgeois author, who had previously been identified with leftist friends, dared to write a play that could be interpreted as an incitement to revolution.[10] The reaction was swift and direct. Although censorship had officially been abolished, it was promptly revived de facto by the Berlin police under the pretext of preventing civil disobedience.[11] In March, 1892, after a period of intense and vehement litigation, the premiere of the dialect version was prohibited; in January, 1893, the modified version suffered the same fate. Not until February 26, 1893, was a performance finally permitted by the *Freie Bühne*—a privately sponsored organization not open to the general public—and in October of the same year this privilege was extended to the Deutsches Theater with the revealing and grotesque justification that the violence-prone segment of the population could not affort the high admission prices! That this solution did not satisfy the more conservative elements of the regime is best evidenced by the fact that Emperor Wilhelm II promptly cancelled his standing subscription to a box in the Deutsches Theater in protest and, subsequently, prevented the award of the Schiller Prize to Hauptmann.[12]

The arguments of both sides in the controversy are still relevant since they bear directly on the interpretation of the play. Hauptmann's counsel argued that *Die Weber* was a work of disinterested art, without propagandistic intent, about an incident from German history—the abortive revolt of a small group of Silesian weavers in 1844. This view is supported by the patently documentary nature of the work. In researching the historical background the author had relied heavily on three sources,[13] and even a superficial comparison of the play with these accounts cannot fail to impress the reader with his remarkable fidelity to the facts and details of the weavers' dire circumstances and their desperate uprising. The prosecution, meanwhile, argued that, while an historical interpretation was not impossible, the disguised intent of the work was an attack on *current* conditions in the weaving industry with the purpose of inciting the workers to revolt. This view too is not farfetched. While it was hardly flattering for the regime to admit it, the weavers' situation around 1890 was almost identical with that of 1844. Their plight had once again become desperate, and the controversy over this burning national issue had found a forum in numerous newspaper and magazine articles.[14] Indeed, Hauptmann himself, in the company of Max Baginski, a socialist reporter, had complemented his formal study of the problem with firsthand observations. He had seen the weavers' suffering with his own eyes: people dying of starvation; small children forced to work long hours from almost the time they learned to walk; a mother and her newborn infant covered with peat litter since they had neither blankets nor clothing to keep them warm; children, up to the ages of six and seven, without even rags to cover their nakedness—in short, conditions even worse than he had described them in the play.[15] Even if he had wished to remain objective (not a typical requirement for a work of art such as he claimed he had written), he could hardly have prevented his emotions from insinuating themselves into his play. Besides, his dedication of the work to his father, Robert Hauptmann, testified to a deep personal sympathy: "If I dedicate this drama to you, dear father, it is from feelings which you know, and which require no analysis here. Your story about grandfather, who as a young man, a poor weaver, sat behind the loom like those I have portrayed, became the germ of my work. Whether it now proves capable of life or is inwardly rotten, it is still the best that 'a poor man such as Hamlet' is able to give" (1:321).

Further complicating the interpretation of *Die Weber* is its surprising fifth act. After four acts which seem to build toward the inevitability of revolution, a new character is introduced who goes completely counter to that expectation. Old Hilse, furthermore, who appears on stage immediately after an act largely devoted to criticism of the shams of orthodox religion, introduces a strong religious note which can be perceived as quite genuine and sincere. Reactions to Hilse have been almost as varied—and predictable—as the political and religious persuasions of those who reveal them. Reduced to their essence, the most frequently encountered attitudes can be summarized as follows: (1) Hauptmann wanted things both ways; shocked by the direction his play seemed to be taking, he added a fifth act as a diplomatic compromise which would spare him the full wrath of the authorities while permitting him to speak out on a subject of wide concern. (2) Old Hilse, his attitude, and his death, are a clear confirmation of the play's Marxist orientation. A victim of bourgeois religion ("the opium of the people"), Hilse has been duped into exchanging a measure of social and economic justice in this life for the empty promise of a life to come. He is portrayed as a living anachronism destroyed by the very revolution he sought to impede. (3) Hilse represents a basic outlook on life that Hauptmann himself shared; i.e., human subjugation by a fate too powerful to be resisted and redemption at the price of prolonged and intense suffering. While it is possible that Hauptmann shared, to a greater or lesser extent, all (or any combination of) these viewpoints, a brief examination of each of them in order should enhance our understanding of both play and author.

(1) Almost from the beginning of his career Hauptmann was accused of compromise, vacillation, and opportunism. Conrad Alberti, a contemporary literary agitator and self-styled revolutionary, describes him as a man without character or deep convictions, the son of a prosperous bourgeois merchant who sets his sail to the most convenient wind: "He tries to do right by everyone, so that everyone will side with him: In *Die Weber* a thoroughgoing socialist, in *Einsame Menschen* an anarchist, in *Hannele* a sanctimonious pietist. . . . Everywhere he allows only himself to be performed, all he wants is to make an impression, capture souls, 'develop' himself from ever new aspects."[16] If we subtract the strident polemical tone from this description, an unflattering element of truth still persists. Certainly in his personal life—the circumstances of his first marriage, his sudden change of allegiance from Holz to Brahm, his later dealings with his publisher, and his stance vis-à-vis the Nazis—elements of compromise, vacillation, and opportunism are hard to deny. The question remains whether these traits had a detrimental effect on his work in general and the final act of *Die Weber* in particular? As Klaus Müller-Salget has shown, especially in reference to some of the later plays, Hauptmann had a tendency to tone down and defuse potentially inflammatory political references from early drafts before making them public.[17] Once he had committed himself to the depiction and interpretation of a specific historical event, however, his options were severely limited. Like Büchner in *Danton's Tod,* he seems to have concluded that base feelings of revenge on the part of the insurgents were in danger of smothering the true revolutionary spirit. As Fontane saw it, Hauptmann's artistic integrity was too great to permit him to end a tragedy with petty "mirror smashing" or on a note of "pure negation." Act V, therefore, is a makeshift solution, but a necessary one: "That something arose from this, which is revolutionary and anti-revolutionary at the same time, we must accept. . . ."[18]

(2) If we recall the central position Hauptmann held in German literary history for more than a generation, it is hardly surprising that Marxist-oriented critics have also tried to salvage a modicum of encouragement from *Die Weber*. At the conclusion of the play, according to

Ursula Münchow, "the solidarity of the weavers stands powerfully and indisputably against their exploiters."[19] For Eberhard Hilscher, Hilse's death indicates Hauptmann's belief "that in life-and-death decisions one may not stand aside and that, in the final analysis, one cannot escape the fate of one' own class."[20] Other critics see Hilse as the incarnation of his creator's alleged views on religion as "the opium of the people"[21] and regret the play's imbalance between the suppressed and suffering *Elendsgestalten* (i.e., "figures of misery") and the forces of revolt and rebellion.[22] While it may not be possible to completely refute such an identification with socialism on the basis of the author's own remarks—elicited post factum, they *could* be seen as an effort to extricate himself from a difficult situation—it will also not do to ignore them or the literary aegis under which the play was written. Hauptmann himself was unequivocal in this regard. "If I stood close to socialism," he reminisced, "I nevertheless did not regard myself as a socialist. It was the uniqueness of my being upon which I insisted and which I defended with desperate courage against everything" (7:1047). The impetus for the work was personal (i.e., family experience) and literary. He wished to "return to dialect its dignity" (7:1079) and to be "the initiator of a new era" by creating a new genre, the social drama (7:1078). Whatever it may imply about his character, his attitude was that of a literary craftsman—as his remarks to an interviewer make drastically clear: "As deeply, for example, as I was moved by the sufferings of a weaver, when I conceived the plan for my play; when I had once set to work, I only saw . . . the wonderful material. . . ."[23] As a writer associated with the Naturalist movement, he shared that movement's obsession with formal experimentation for which subject matter—including "proletarian" motifs—was grist for the mill.[24]

Even within the context of the play itself it is difficult to argue for a socialist interpretation of Act V. Hilse is not (and certainly not only) a religious fanatic. Unlike Bäcker and Jäger, he has been taught by firsthand experience in battle how futile and pathetic the weavers' revolt is in the face of superior armed forces (Cf.1:473). While one may argue that it is the moral obligation of an oppressed proletariat to *attempt* to overthrow its capitalist exploiters despite impossible odds, the irony remains that Hilse is not only the most religious, but also the most pragmatic of the weavers. We have no way of judging the correctness of his religious views, but the history of the event Hauptmann is describing confirms Hilse's political prescience since the revolt was brutally crushed with no appreciable benefit to the rebels.

(3) "Hauptmann, though leftish in his sympathies, never subscribed to any party line or believed in political action as efficacious for the solving of basic human problems."[25] Like his predecessor Friedrich Hebbel and unlike his successor Bertolt Brecht or the Naturalists themselves, he was attracted by the transcendent, metaphysical problems of the basic human predicament: suffering, fate, and the possibility of spiritual catharsis. Such works as *Michael Kramer, Rose Bernd,* and *Veland* leave little doubt as to this basic predisposition; the only question is whether or not it can be legitimately invoked in an interpretation of *Die Weber.* A number of prominent scholars believe it can. For Karl S. Guthke and Kurt May, this metaphysical stance is evident at least as early as *Die Weber,* and Benno von Wiese sees traces of it even in *Vor Sonnenaufgang.*[26] Difficulties arise only when one equates Hauptmann too pedantically with Hilse (actually, Weinhold is a much more accurate portrayal of the author as a young man), and if one fails to draw any distinction between Hauptmann the artist and the man. Two questions then present themselves. If, as Paul Schlenther observed soon after its appearance, the play is a "modern fate drama,"[27] why does Hauptmann take such pains to describe its milieu in the modern terms of a strictly deterministic environment? And if he is as strongly opposed to orthodox religion as he appears to be from the events depicted in Act IV, why is Hilse made to epitomize such religion? The answer to the first question seems to be that Hauptmann saw heredity and environment as mere expressions of a much more profound and mysterious fate; the answer to the second, that Hilse's intense religiosity cannot be compared with the superficial dogmatism of Pastor Kittelhaus, since Hilse's seeming dogmatism is coincidental and a requirement of realism. Given Hilse's social status, it would have been completely out of character for him to express his religious feelings in a highly original manner.[28] As a literary craftsman, Hauptmann was indebted to the techniques of Naturalism, but its shallow materialistic outlook failed to satisfy him as a human being. Like *Das Friedensfest,* therefore, the play is a dissertation on the banality of the concepts of optimism and pessimism. On a sociopolitical level, history supplies the pessimistic outcome; whereas on a metaphysical level the radiant character of Hilse, in spite (or because?) of his death, provides a ray of hope—if only because fate seems to take an active interest in its subjects.

Hanneles Himmelfahrt

If *Die Weber* had seemed uncomfortably ambiguous to many so-
cialist-oriented critics, there is little vacillation in their appraisal of
Hanneles Himmelfahrt [The Assumption of Hannele]. This perennially
popular *Traumdichtung* ("Dream Play"), written in 1893 and performed
in Paris and New York as early as the following year, appeared at first
glance to be a complete betrayal of both Naturalist and socialist ideals.
A complex amalgam of realistic description and fairy-tale elements; of
psychological nuance and emotional intensity which, occasionally,
lapses into sentimentality, the two-act drama both provoked and
saddened Franz Mehring, the leading socialist critic of the day. "Never
before," he wrote, "have we been condemned to witness with our own
eyes such a great abuse of such a great talent."[29] Instead of depicting
suffering and injustice with a view toward provoking social action that
would alleviate them, Hauptmann had accepted—indeed glorified as
virtues—poverty and pain.

Biographically, *Hannele* is rooted in the author's Lederose period; a
time when he was strongly enmeshed in problems of puberty and
religion. At that time his aunt and uncle had bought a poor, sickly,
lice-infested girl of seven from her drunken stonemason father and
taken her into their home. Hauptmann's very personal involvement in
the transaction is expressed in his recollection: "I understood that she
was intended to replace me" (7:771). A second model for the play's title
role was the thirteen-year-old daughter of a poor widow in Reichenbach
whom the author had met on his research trip for *Die Weber* and whom
he later occasionally favored with presents.[30] That the subject matter of
Hannele, including the erotically motivated dream and "salvation" of a
poor dying child, preoccupied Hauptmann at least as early as 1887 is
evident in "Die Mondbraut" [The Moonbride], a ballad from *Das bunte
Buch* (4:72–75). With the exception of a stronger emphasis on her
religiosity in the play, the substance of *Hannele*'s story is very similar to
that of the ballad.

The play opens on a scrupulously Naturalistic note. The setting is a
village poorhouse, populated by an assortment of interesting and
mildly amusing characters thrown together by the desire for protection
from the December cold as much as for a few crumbs to eat and the
chance for a little companionship. Into these dismal surroundings
Hauptmann introduces Hannele Mattern, who, driven to desperation

by her abusive, constantly drunk stepfather, had tried to drown herself in the icy village pond, only to be rescued at the last minute by Gottwald, the local teacher. In a series of actions which make more dramatic than logical sense, he first took her home to his warm house, where his wife dressed her in dry clothes, and then, in spite of her obviously precarious condition, carried her over to the poorhouse where the inmates could look after her. The remainder of the first act is largely taken up with visits by the local physician, Wachler, *Amtsvorsteher* ("head official") Berger, and a series of visions in which the fourteen-year-old girl is confronted in turn by her brutal stepfather, a woman's figure that Hannele takes to be her mother, and three beautiful male angels who speak to her in musically accentuated verse.

The second act dispenses almost completely with the Naturalistic trappings of the first, concentrating instead on the depiction of the feverish fantasy world of the dying Hannele. Vacillating between earthly fear and heavenly bliss, she receives a series of visitors: a small, hunchbacked tailor who brings her her bridal clothes and a pair of glass slippers which legitimize her as the secret princess of the realm; a black angel of death; Gottwald and his school children; and, finally her "bridegroom," a stranger with the combined features of Gottwald and Christ, who confronts Mattern with his crimes against Hannele and drives him to suicide. The ending of the second act almost, but not quite, parallels that of the first. Both end with angelic music, but just before the final curtain the scene reverts abruptly from fantasy to cold reality: the lights go up, we find ourselves back in the harsh poorhouse atmosphere, and Dr. Wachler, bending over Hannele's inert, emaciated body with his stethoscope, confirms that she has died. A third act, depicting Hannele's afterlife as an angel, her reunion with her mother, and her heavenly marriage to Gottwald, was deleted by Hauptmann before the play's premiere (Cf. 9:744–67).

Seen in retrospect and in the context of his earlier and later work, Hauptmann's *Hannele* now seems a logical stage in the organic development of his talent. On the one hand, with its emphasis on an exact reproduction of the crass reality of the poorhouse and its concern for such problems as alcoholism and child abuse the play is artistically compatible with the Naturalism of *Vor Sonnenaufgang*. On the other hand, particularly in the dream sequences and hallucinations which make up more than half of *Hannele* there is an unmistakable predilection for those lyrically mystical elements that attract the author more and more as time goes on. While the coexistence of material and mystical forces is certainly not new to him (as *Bahnwärter Thiel* testifies), he had never before so carefully balanced them against each other in a play. That this drama is, nonetheless, not fragmented into spiritual and materialistic components, is again due to Hauptmann's skill in creating multifaceted characters, his subtle psychological motivation, and his use of a few very basic symbols.

Again the lesser characters from the lower classes are masterfully executed. To mention just one example, Pleschke—like Hopslabaer in *Vor Sonnenaufgang* a simple-minded stutterer with a goiter—seems to have very little function in the plot. He does, however, contribute to the general ambience of barely concealed cruelty which is one of the wellsprings of Hauptmann's work. By making Pleschke's stutter humorous and by ridiculing it through Hete's cold-hearted imitation (1:552) he not only intensifies the atmosphere of cruelty on the stage but also involves the audience in uneasy complicity.

More interesting, of course, is the character of Hannele herself. Since she is an idealization, Hauptmann has spared her the Naturalistic verisimilitude of the heavy dialect one would expect a girl of her station to use, but he took great pains with the psychological motivation of her character. The fact that she is an illegitimate child (perhaps the daughter of *Amtsvorsteher* Berger himself, as village gossip suggests [1:558]) might certainly have contributed to the discord with her stepfather and could have done very little to enhance her own self-image. In one sense, her dreams and hallucinations on her deathbed are quite realistic. As Hauptmann pointed out, "all her visions can be explained on a purely pathological basis."[31] It is through them and the strength of her wish projections (i.e., for beautiful clothes, admiration of her peers, love of Gottwald) that we see into the secret recesses of her soul and come to understand the full extent of her suffering. The fact that her dreams abound in references to Christian myth and German fairy tales (i.e., Frau Holle's well, Snow White's glass coffin, and Cinderella's slipper) is actually a realistic touch: these are the elements of her sparse "education."

Hannele is more than a "case history" of an individual, and her dreams are more than material for a (pre-)Freudian analysis. As a character type she is the first hesitant example in a series of erotically excited teen-age girls who attracted Hauptmann and appear in his work from now on. But she is also more than a type. As Leroy R. Shaw points out, her situation is "a symbolic representation of the general human predicament."[32] Delivered into the poorhouse—itself symbolic of the world as "vale of tears," she witnesses in her soul the primordial struggle between personifications of evil and good (Mattern/Satan vs. Gottwald/Christ) and achieves heavenly salvation through the earthly suffering that costs her her life. As Hauptmann confirmed in 1894, "Earthly pain created heavenly bliss; earthly poverty [created] fairy-tale riches. . . ."[33]

Even if we were to take the more pessimistic view that, by concluding the play with Dr. Wachler's clinical confirmation of her death, Hauptmann is implying that Hannele has been duped by her faith, her religion would nonetheless have served a purpose: as in the case of Hilse, it certainly made her death easier—for her and, therefore, for the audience.

Perhaps more important than *Hannele's* content for documenting Hauptmann's growing estrangement from Naturalism are the formal innovations of the play. Of these the most significant for his future work is one we have already touched upon: the use of the dream as a means of expanding reality in both a literal and a formal sense. For Hauptmann the dream was an important source of truth and "what he was striving for was an equilibrium to which life and dream would contribute equally, no longer each to the exclusion of the other, but also not unbalanced by a denial of the reality of the waking life."[34] Even though the dream segments in *Hannele* are formally segregated from the depictions of empirical reality (in later works the lines of demarcation become increasingly blurred), they signal a break with one of the most cherished tenets of Naturalism: that an author is limited in his depictions to the physical world around him. In addition, the introduction of highly imaginative dreams and visions leads easily to a number of other deviations from the Naturalist ideal. An epic element—in which Hannele becomes in essence the "narrator" of her dreams—is introduced; lines of poetry, fairy-tale elements, and biblical allusions counterbalance the more starkly realistic passages, and, in general, the author permits himself a greater latitude for experimentation. For Hauptmann this included the use of Baroque (i.e., chorus) and even medieval (i.e., the "disputatio" between "Mattern" and "Gottwald") dramatic forms. The end result is a play which—the presence of some of Hauptmann's most Naturalistic scenes notwithstanding—comes very close to fin-de-siècle Neoromanticism.[35]

Chapter Five
Shades of Comedy

Der Biberpelz

Der Biberpelz: Eine Diebskomödie [The Beaver Coat: A Thieves' Comedy] remains "the most illustrious and successful comedy of modern German dramatic literature."[1] Written in 1892–93 and rather inexplicably cleared by the censor for its premiere in the Deutsches Theater on September 21, 1893, it is generally recognized as one of the three great German comedies of all time—Lessing's *Minna von Barnhelm* and Kleist's *Der zerbrochene Krug* [The Broken Jug] providing the distinguished company. Like these predecessors, it is a *Charakterkomödie*. It is more dependent on the skillful delineation of interesting characters than upon intricacies of plot; and its innumerable stagings, wide use in the classroom, and three film versions have guaranteed it a place among the most widely known and loved German cultural achievements of the last century.

The play opens "somewhere near Berlin" around the end of the eighties in the kitchen of Frau Wolff, a hard-working, well-liked washerwoman. Together with her husband, she has just snared a deer and, in a comic bargaining session which leaves no doubt as to the quality of her wit, tenacity, and verbal persuasiveness, she manages to sell it very advantageously to Wulkow, an older, somewhat disreputable Spree river boatman who has obviously had similar "business" dealings with her before. In the ensuing small talk involving Wulkow's rheumatism, his need for a fur coat, and the chance remark of Leontine, Frau Wolff's seventeen-year-old daughter, that her elderly employer Krüger has a beautiful new beaver coat, we detect the inception of an even more profitable transaction. Just after Wulkow's departure, Frau Wolff is forced to receive two more late-night visitors: Motes—a shady character who calls himself a writer—and his equally unpleasant wife. By dropping threats to the effect that nothing would give him greater pleasure than to report poachers to the authorities, he blackmails

Mother Wolff into giving him eggs and bread on credit. When she is finally rid of these unwelcome guests, she has a moment alone with her husband Julius in which, plying him with drink and argumentation too strong for his feeble mentality, she persuades him of the advantages that selling Krüger's coat to Wulkow would have: they could pay off their debt on the house, take out another small loan to add a room or two for summer tourists, and, in that way, do something for the future of their daughters. In the meantime, however, she has another task for her husband. Leontine has threatened to give up her job because her employer has ordered her to bring a stack of firewood into the house before quitting work for the day. Frau Wolff sends Julius off with a sled to steal the wood, which has been left in the street, and the fact that *Amtsdiener* ("beadle") Mitteldorff bungles onto the scene only adds spice to the enterprise. She enlists him as an unwitting accomplice by having him hold a lantern while she and Julius make their preparations for the theft!

Act II takes place in the office of Baron von Wehrhahn, a pompous, monocled, ultraconservative local official with an abiding hatred for democrats and critics of the status quo. Through his scribe Glasenapp and the informer Motes he would like nothing better than to convict Krüger—and especially the old man's tenant Dr. Fleischer—of treasonable acts. When Krüger arrives to notify the official of the theft of his firewood and to demand that Mother Wolff make restitution (since her daughter's irresponsibility made the theft possible), the washerwoman is summoned. She appears immediately from the laundry room where she is working for Wehrhahn but resolutely refuses Krüger's demand. Von Wehrhahn, who heartily dislikes the old "liberal," now insists that he bring his charges in writing. And in a remark to Motes he wearily confides that the only thing that makes it possible for him to continue wasting his time on such trifles is the knowledge that he is engaged in a noble struggle on behalf of the "highest values of the nation!" (1:517).

The third act returns us to Mother Wolff's home. As it begins, she is counting the money Wulkow has paid her for Krüger's coat, and when her husband appears she sends him off to bury it in a pouch in the stable. Daughter Adelheid, who makes allusions to the new firewood, receives a box on the ears for her impertinence. Finally, too, we meet Dr. Fleischer who has brought his delicate small son for a boat ride. Mother Wolff warns him of Motes's intrigues and the two commiserate over the Krüger thefts. After Fleischer's departure the old man himself appears, and there is a touching reconciliation scene during which Krüger expresses his willingness to take Leontine back into his employ—at a higher salary than before. The act ends on a note of solidarity. While angrily waving about a piece of his own (stolen) wood, Krüger complains bitterly about the thefts and gains Mother Wolff's expression of unstinting support of his fervent desire to see the criminals behind bars.

In the fourth act all the protagonists are brought together in Wehrhahn's office for the first and last time: Mother Wolff and Adelheid to provide him with a false clue as to the whereabouts of the stolen fur; Fleischer to give honest testimony regarding the case; Krüger to insist on his rights, and even Wulkow to register the birth of a daughter. By this time, however, Wehrhahn's preoccupation with Fleischer's alleged political transgressions has become a blind obsession—in spite of the fact that, thanks largely to the tactician Mother Wolff, Motes has been effectively muzzled. He is neither willing nor able to pursue the very real thieves of Krüger's property, and his admiration for Mother Wolff as an honest, decent citizen knows no bounds. Fleischer's testimony that he saw a boatman wearing a fur coat suspiciously like the stolen one is defused by Wehrhahn and the recipient of the stolen goods himself. Asked if it is not unusual for a boatman to own such an expensive coat, Wulkow modestly replies in the negative; after all, he himself has one.

The play ends with none of the issues resolved. Krüger's property is never restored, and, at least in Wehrhahn's eyes, Frau Wolff's reputation has risen while Fleischer's has suffered further damage. Justice, it appears, is indeed blind!

The success of *Der Biberpelz* undoubtedly owes a great deal to its author's familiarity with its physical locale, the historical circumstances of the era it portrays, and the real people who served as models for its characters. Something of the transition from rural to metropolitan values can be felt in the atmosphere of the small community that is being gradually absorbed by the rapidly expanding city of Berlin. The lure of the bright lights, easy money, and relaxed morality are reflected both in Mother Wolff's wish to see her daughters become actresses and in Leontine's threat that she will go to the city to work as a seamstress. While neither of these professions was especially conducive to the morality of single girls who practiced them alone in the big city, the former, at least, promised greater financial reward. For the knowledge-able, Hauptmann also very succinctly suggests the historical atmo-sphere of his play. The time is specifically given as "Septennatskampf gegen Ende der achtziger Jahre" ("Septenat struggle toward the end of the eighties" [1:483]). This phrase refers to Bismarck's tenacious efforts to maintain funding for his peacetime army for another seven years and (as happened in 1887) to get permission to increase the size of that army. Opponents of these measures, such as liberals, democrats, and socialists, were considered enemies of the Reich. Like Fleischer and Krüger, they were ruthlessly spied upon and harassed by public offi-cials, who were frequently appointed on the basis of social position rather than ability, who placed loyalty to the regime above all else, and who saw themselves as the direct representatives of the Kaiser.[2]

Hauptmann's knowledge of these conditions was direct and per-sonal. During his stay in Erkner he met the people and experienced some of the events that later found their way into his play. Like Fleischer, he was a young outsider of precarious health whose mail (e.g., the Socialist periodical *Die Neue Zeit* [The New Age]) attracted the attention of a local "political Hotspur," a certain Oscar von Buße, the prototype of Wehrhahn (7:1043–44). It was to the pompous, disdainful von Buße—who, like Wehrhahn, considered himself to be the local "king"—that Hauptmann (like Wulkow) had to report the birth of his sons and to whom (like Adelheid) he brought a suspicious package of clothing he had found in the forest (7:1044). In Erkner, too, he met the models for Krüger (his landlord Nikolaus Lassen), for Motes (Cf. 7:1045), and the Wolff family. Mother Wolff is based on Marie Heinze, Hauptmann's own washerwoman, and Ida Heinze, a daughter, worked for years in the Hauptmann household. Naturally, both people and events underwent artistic refinement. Mrs. Heinze was no thief, and some of the events depicted in the autobiography must have seemed too farfetched even for inclusion in a comedy. For example, even though an orange is rather mysteriously featured in the play (1:522), the anecdote about Hauptmann's juggling with oranges as alleged practice for bomb-throwing is mercifully omitted.[3]

Like any successful work of art *Der Biberpelz* is multileveled and multifaceted. And, while a fuller discussion of certain aspects of its content is best postponed until we deal with the tragicomedy *Der rote Hahn* [The Red Cock], essentially a continuation of Mother Wolff's saga, a few remarks about the play's political nature must be interspersed here. *Der Biberpelz* (like *Die Weber*) is a "politicized" play which does not express the specific outlook of any particular party. Although she has her own private "share the wealth plan" (i.e., she is not opposed to "sharing" Krüger's wealth), Mother Wolff is hardly a socialist. Neither hungry, in need, exploited, nor consciously aligned with the proletariat—nor with the more theoretical views of Fleischer and Krüger, for that matter—she is an overpowering woman who knows what she wants and is not overly fastidious in her means for obtaining it. As a satirical figure, she functions on a specific and a general level. Specifically, she embodies the materialistic outlook of the Wilhelminian Age when religion was no longer the restraining influence it had been, when a shallow rationalism glorified the instincts, and when a rapidly expanding industrialization was leading inevitably to a "consumer society" and "upward mobility." In addition to being a reflection of the zeitgeist, however, she has also become the embodiment of a "social satire of an all-embracing variety."[4] As Hermann W. Weigand succinctly sums it up: "The general upshot of the spectacle is: such is life in a competitive modern society. We distinctly feel the career of this washerwoman as a symbol of the same drive and of analogous processes in all strata of our society. Sansara—they would call it in India."[5] Thus, while a knowledge of the age in which it was written can enhance its appreciation, such is not absolutely essential, and in a general way the play is still relevant today.

Albeit with somewhat stronger reservations, a similar case can be made for Hauptmann's humor, i.e., his handling of the intangibles of language. To an even greater degree than most Naturalist dramas *Der Biberpelz* is impervious to adequate translation. Not only does Hauptmann adhere to his usual practice of individualizing his characters by having them speak in their own, unmistakable linguistic "tone" and rhythm, but—with the major exception of Fleischer—they all labor, to a greater or lesser extent, under the comic burden of a potpourri of dialectal inflections as well. The would-be actresses Adelheid and Leontine speak the dialect of Berlin (while complaining of their father's "uneducated" language!); Frau Wolff speaks in a combination of Berlin jargon and Silesian expressions; Julius and Wulkow include elements of *Plattdeutsch* in their speech; and Krüger contributes more than a touch of the dialect of Saxony.[6] The result—especially when several people try to speak at the same time—is a delightful and inimitable Babel with the serious undertone evoked by that biblical name: the ultimate futility of human attempts at communication.

Another source of frustration for translators of Hauptmann are the names of his characters. A full investigation into this seemingly minor aspect of his art would require a study at least the length of this book, and even then it could not possibly exhaust the topic.[7] As Paul Fechter observed more than half a century ago, "There is no other writer who . . . perceives the sound of names as sensitively as Hauptmann. The characters of his dramas possess, without exception, names which belong to them absolutely, which coincide with their essence, in whose sound every bit of conscious work, of 'literature,' is eradicated."[8] It might be added that these names are invariably existent (rather than fanciful inventions) and their choice depends on a variety of circumstances. In some instances (e.g., the frequent Maries, Augustes, and their variants) Hauptmann appears to be primarily interested in paying disguised tribute to a member of his family or someone close to him. For example, during his student days in Breslau, a friend, Max Fleischer, played a major role in rescuing him from the degradation of his impoverished existence (Cf. 7:864–66). It would not seem surprising if the choice of that surname for the morally and intellectually most attractive character in *Der Biberpelz* were a surreptitious homage to this friend. Since, in this instance, we are dealing with a comedy, however, and since Hauptmann was perfectly aware of the comic potential of names, most of the names in the play are allusive. Thus, Glasenapp and Mitteldorf add an intangible quality of humorous insufficiency to the characters of their bearers, and the names Adelheid and Leontine suggest something of the pretentious and aggressive social ambition of the mother who named them.

Another category includes the so-called *sprechende Namen*: names which express, either directly or in slightly disguised fashion, certain qualities of their bearers—an old tradition of comic literature. Here Krüger (dialect: Krieger="fighter") is a case in point, as are especially Wehrhahn and Mutter Wolff. And, while we may not be willing to go as far in our interpretation as Jean Jofen who claims "the washerwoman 'wolf' in *Der Biberpelz* awakens the association with the she-wolf, which suckled Romulus and Remus,"[9] her name leaves little doubt that she will triumph over an opponent whose name derives from that of a mere fowl. The name Wehrhahn consists of two components: *Wehr* with militaristic overtones such as "defense," and *Hahn,* a "cock" or "rooster." A strutting, vain, foolish cockalorum like Wehrhahn is no match for a "wolf in sheep's clothing" like Mother Wolff—especially when Wehrhahn insists on reserving that role for the innocent Fleischer (Cf. 1:533).

The use of animal names and animal imagery—like the derivation of much of the humor from low and stock characters—suggests the venerable roots of Hauptmann's comedy. Certainly it owes something to the realistic, mimetic tradition of the European eighteenth century, to Molière and to Kleist's *Der zerbrochene Krug;* but beyond that it is reminiscent of Aristophanes and of even older, archetypal drama in which human beings hid behind animal masks: "In *Der Biberpelz* and *Der rote Hahn* I inadvertently reached into the area of mimic folk humor,"[10] the author was later to confess. Just how deeply he reached is suggested by elements of humor that derive their effectiveness from basically cruel situations (e.g., Mitteldorf's mental deficiency and propensity for drowning his troubles in alcohol, or Krüger's deafness) or sadistically funny statements like Wehrhahn's comment on Fleischer's diabetic condition: "Let him sweat syrup" (1:505). That Hauptmann sensed this relationship between cruelty and comedy seems clear from Fleischer's remarks about the theft of the Krüger coat: "The little people [i.e., Krüger and his wife] were very proud of it.—That is: of course I laughed about it to myself. When something like that is discovered, it always strikes one as being funny" (1:526).

As in the case of the other great German comedies, *Der Biberpelz* owes its effectiveness to such counterpointing of humor and serious undertones. Theft is not innately funny, and the intrigue which Motes and Wehrhahn direct against Krüger and Fleischer has the potential for serious consequences. With time, indeed, Hauptmann himself saw the play more and more in terms of his prevailing conviction that true comedy is invariably tragicomedy.[11]

The real novelty of *Der Biberpelz,* judging from the puzzled reactions of contemporary audiences and critics, lay more in matters of form than in content. Professional critics, educated in the Classical tradition of Schiller and the rigid dramaturgical norms of Gustav Freytag, were disturbed by alleged weaknesses of composition (such as the repetitiousness of three thefts); the lack of character development; the rather loose linking of scenes, and the lack of a traditional denouement.[12] The play's "open ending"—occurring at the high point of the action and in complete disregard for the age-old tradition that the guilty must be punished—was so unusual that the audience remained seated in expectation of a fifth act which would bring clarity and justice.[13] The fact that these innovations were considered so daring when the play first appeared is another tribute to Hauptmann's modernity. While still largely beholden to the unities of time and place, he relied more heavily on a unity of character than of action and preferred truth to moralizing. Although not structured along traditional lines, the play shows evidence of having been planned and written with a great deal of care and attention to detail. It deviates from the traditional pyramid schema of Classical drama (i.e., five acts with the highpoint in the third) in favor of a form more reminiscent of a carousel; act endings are carefully worked out for maximum theatrical effectiveness and skillfully integrated into the overall design, and a strong feeling of suspense is maintained not only in regard to the solutions of the thefts and Wehrhahn's political machinations but also in the way characters (especially Fleischer) are talked about long before they appear on stage.[14] The sense of unity and artistic integrity is further enhanced by the principles of symmetry, parallelism, and repetition which are basic to the play's structure. Thus the scene shifts back and forth symmetrically from the Wolff home to the office of Wehrhahn; the plot zigzags between the comic thefts and serious political accusations, and Frau Wolff's natural superiority as an individual is strongly challenged by the state which Wehrhahn represents. Even the repetitious thefts, which occur offstage and thus remain somewhat abstract, contribute to both the symmetry and the humor of the play. On the one hand, the repetition serves to underscore the uniqueness of Mother Wolff's nature. A woman satisfied with the deer or the stolen firewood would have been too nondescript to hold our attention. Like other great comic figures, she is larger than life and filled with an exuberance that drives her to ever greater risks. On the other hand, repetition itself is indigenous to comedy, and laughter is a reflex that can be elicited by simple, repetitive schemata.[15]

That the play's ending was also criticized and misunderstood is due to Hauptmann's bold departure from the venerable tradition that villains must be punished and justice served. That Mother Wolff

escapes punishment introduces an element of relativity into the definition of legality (who is the greater "criminal," she or the tyrant
Wehrhahn?) and an element of reality into the plot (real criminals are
not always apprehended). Indeed, given the nature of the protagonists,
the satirical tendency of the play, and the Naturalist requirement that
art should be a faithful reflection of life, Hauptmann's solution is
eminently successful. By ending the play at the highpoint of his
heroine's deception—the ultimate triumph of appearance over
reality—he makes an ironic statement concerning the validity of a state
run by the likes of Wehrhahn and provides an ending that is both
"open" and "closed": open in the sense that the various elements of the
plot are not neatly tied together as in traditional drama; closed, in that
we are left with no illusions—Frau Wolff will continue with her petty
thievery, Wehrhahn will continue to misjudge those around him, and
life will go on as before.[16]

Der rote Hahn

It has become customary to treat the tragicomedy *Der rote Hahn* [The
Red Cock] together with *Der Biberpelz,* although it was not written
until 1900/1901 and lacks the vitality and effervescent humor of its
predecessor. Again the drama is located "somewhere near Berlin" and
the time is indicated by a contemporary political reference: the era of
"struggle over the Lex Heinze," an allusion to repressive attempts at
censorship at the turn of the century.[17] Although the plot continues the
description of the fortunes of the Wolff family, the intervening decade
has brought almost catastrophic change. We no longer sense the
redeeming atmosphere of nature in the new setting. Life has become
increasingly materialistic, burdensome, and mean, and we find ourselves amidst a radically changed cast of characters. The sickly outsider
Dr. Fleischer has been replaced by a parallel figure, Dr. Boxer, a
muscular Jewish physician with a physique worthy of his name; the
liberal Krüger has been eliminated (as have Motes, Mitteldorf, and
Wulkow); Julius Wolff has died; Adelheid and Leontine have not
become actresses; and Wehrhahn has assumed a much smaller role and a
new mode of speech—he now speaks in strong Berlin accents. Even the
heroine has changed almost beyond recognition. By her own admission
she is "no longer Mother Wolff!" (2:15). The intervening ten years have

aged her disproportionately, and her improved financial situation has been counterbalanced by a loss of health and self-assurance and by a new husband of dubious worth. Indeed, it is an indication of just how low she has fallen when we recall that she had earlier dismissed this man with the telling name of Fielitz ("miser") as "the lousy Fielitz-shoemaker" (1:489) and police spy.

Albeit somewhat enigmatic, the plot of the four-act play is more rudimentary than that of *Der Biberpelz*. Again there are autobiographical sources; in particular, a visit to the community of Kagel near Berlin in 1894 and stories about mysterious fires and insurance frauds which came to Hauptmann's attention at that time.[18]

By now, Mother Wolff/Fielitz has seemingly realized her dreams. Together with her new husband she has achieved solid middle-class security and respectability and has married her daughter Adelheid to a ruthless and successful businessman named Schmarowski *(Schmarot-zer* = "parasite"). For whatever reason—force of habit or hubris—she decided to continue her social climb by delivering up her own house to the "red cock" i.e., by committing arson. Outwardly successful, she collects seven thousand marks from the insurance company and can participate in the building speculation of her son-in-law. Although the crime is less than perfect (the blacksmith Langheinrich has found a piece of the fuse she used to set the fire while she and her husband were away in Berlin—and is in a position to blackmail her), she manages to encourage Wehrhahn in his suspicion that the arson is the work of Gustav Rauchhaupt, the weak-minded son of a former local gendarme. Her suggestion to the father that his son is better off committed to an insane asylum for the crime, where he will at least have his three square meals a day, rings hollow; and her own death, soon after this confrontation and in the presence of Dr. Boxer and her husband—who completely ignores her demise—seems almost coincidental.

Stripped of its "epic" discussions and conversations and reduced to a minimal plot outline in this way, the problematic aspects of *Der rote Hahn* become especially striking. Mother Wolff has progressed from relatively minor crimes, committed as much out of natural exuberance as malice, to criminal, even despicable, acts. Along the way she has also lost that metaphysical surefootedness described so well in Kleist's *Marionettentheater;* has fallen from grace; and, perhaps, has died in uneasy atonement for her sin. On the whole, the trend is away from comedy and, despite a few mildly funny encounters, toward tragedy; a tragedy, however, that is very much dependent on our recollection of Mother Wolff's vital *Biberpelz* persona for its full impact.

Until recently, and even more so than in the case of *Der Biberpelz*, the tendency has been to stress the political aspects of the drama. But while it is true that Hauptmann touches upon several typical facets of the sociopolitical zeitgeist (e.g., anti-Semitism, the collusion of church and state, and excesses of the capitalist mentality), an exclusively political interpretation is unsatisfactory. For Marxists the problem is again particularly acute. The mere fact that Mother Wolff's material advancement is not accompanied by an improvement in the quality of her life is itself a defect when viewed from this perspective.

The extent to which the two plays—*Biberpelz* and *Roter Hahn*—both attracted and irritated the Marxists, can, perhaps, best be illustrated by the reaction of Bertolt Brecht. As a young man Brecht seems to have had a great deal of respect for Hauptmann and for those contributions of Naturalism that anticipated his concept of epic theater. Later, after his own artistic and political credos were more fully developed, his attitude became more ambiguous. For a man who professed faith in the mutability of society Hauptmann's deterministic outlook was anathema.[19] That Brecht nonetheless continued to respect his predecessor's talent is clear from at least two circumstances: the figure of his own Mother Courage owes a great deal to Mother Wolff,[20] and he was sufficiently interested in *Der Biberpelz* and *Der rote Hahn* to rework and combine them for a six-act presentation by the Berliner Ensemble in March, 1951. In a letter to Berthold Viertel he expressed his intention and, coincidentally, the different perspective of Naturalism and Marxism: "We decided to trust Hauptmann completely insofar as his art of observation was concerned (i.e., we investigated the significance of the smallest details and retained them if at all possible). Less trustworthy, however, was his knowledge of the historically essential. We had to bring the workers' movement (social democracy), which Hauptmann almost completely overlooks, into the picture."[21] The changes Brecht undertook—all of them with the intention of emphasizing the role of the workers' movement and the thesis that social conditions can be changed through organized effort—failed to "rescue" Hauptmann's play for Marxism. Instead of living drama the end result was a rather humorless, intellectualized political tract.[22]

If we reject the priority of a modern political interpretation of this kind, how should the two plays be viewed and what, if anything, unites them in artistic cohesion? For Oskar Seidlin, the answer lies in Hauptmann's long-term preoccupation with the concept of matriarchy. Although not the first critic to notice that *Der Biberpelz* deals with this basic Hauptmannian theme, i.e., "How natural *(urwüchsig)* woman is victorious over man,"[23] Seidlin in his ingenious study describes the progress of this archetypal "political" contest, the battle between the sexes, in convincing detail.[24] According to his reading, *Der Biberpelz* represents the triumph of the mother principle. The male characters, all of them physically and/or mentally defective in one way or another,[25] are no match for the rampant female vitality of Mother Wolff who demonstrates effortlessly how "nature triumphs over artifice, life over form, reality over system."[26] In *Der rote Hahn* the situation is gradually reversed, with the main turning point occurring at the time of the fire. New characters, with aggressively masculine names like Boxer and Langheinrich (i.e., "long Henry"—a name with unmistakable sexual overtones) are introduced; the world has fallen into the hands of cold, unscrupulous schemers like Schmarowski, and Mother Wolff and her daughters have changed from aggressors to victims of men.

Seidlin's interpretation—outlined here in only its barest essentials—goes a long way toward explaining the enigma of *Der rote Hahn* and its complementary relationship to *Der Biberpelz*.

Schluck und Jau

In the fall of 1899 Hauptmann diverted a few weeks from more difficult labors to write *Schluck und Jau*, a "*Scherzspiel*," i.e., a comic or farcical play. In contrast to his usual habit he seems bent on circumventing undue audience expectation when he admonishes us to take "this crude little piece for no more than the child of a cheerful whim" (1:1014). Although they represent little more than the conventional apologies familiar from Shakespearian prologues—a form Hauptmann is obviously parodying—these words may have reinforced the notion that the play lacks substance and does not come up to his usual standards. On those occasions when it has been praised it has often been for the wrong reasons. Thus Joseph Gregor calls it "Hauptmann's best . . . comedy" but finds his justification in its emulation of Shakes-

peare.[27] More recently, Hilscher has numbered it among "Hauptmann's more significant works" but places his main stress on the play's
alleged emphasis on social inequality and the unmasking of "the
inhumanity of the feudal lords, who, to pass the time . . . toy with two
poor human beings."[28]

Additional sources of confusion and misunderstanding can be found
in the work's novelty (for Hauptmann) and in the notion (seemingly
encouraged by the author) that it was largely written as a literary
exercise; a bit of "comic relief" from more serious preoccupations and
therefore without any strong personal convictions.

In spite of the Silesian dialect spoken by Schluck and Jau, and in spite
of the picturesque, mythical court at which the action takes place, the
play had little appeal for the two main segments of Hauptmann's
audience. It is neither Naturalistic enough for his earlier admirers nor
sufficiently Romantic for the later, more conservative group which had
so recently been enchanted by *Die versunkene Glocke* [The Sunken
Bell].[29]

Not knowing quite how to approach the play on its own terms,
critics tended to write about its literary sources, a factor which further
emphasized the derivative nature of the work at the expense of its
originality. While Hauptmann seems to have tried to limit this activity
by focusing attention on Shakespeare (especially *The Taming of the
Shrew*), it was soon obvious that he was indebted to a theme so venerable
and widespread as to be virtually archetypal: that of the peasant who is
made king for a day.[30]

The plot of *Schluck und Jau* is simple and direct. A prologue spoken
by a hunter establishes the scene and mood: a banquet hall of a noble
hunting castle, the elegiac tones of fall, and the end of the seasonal
hunt. The play itself opens with a sharply contrasting scene in front of
the castle. The drunken peasant Jau is gesticulating wildly and scream-
ing at the top of his lungs while his friend Schluck tries to placate him
by promising to fetch him another bottle. Before he can set out on his
mission, however, a returning group of impassioned hunters, consisting of Prince Jon Rand and his courtiers, approaches. Offended by the
unsightly drunkards, the prince wants Jau thrown in prison, but his
companion Karl suggests a game which will amuse the court and relieve
the boredom of Jon's sweetheart Sidselill, who is everlastingly deprived
of his company by his passion for hunting. Jau is transferred to a silken

bed in the castle and, when he awakens, is persuaded by the actions of the servants and the connivance of the court that *he* is the prince. Schluck, although never deceived, is dressed in the clothing of Frau Adeluz, Sidselill's companion, pretending to be Jau's wife. He cooperates reluctantly, in order not to incur the wrath of his captors, and his artistic instincts lead him to try to make the best of a very bad role. After some initial confusion, Jau begins to live his new life with a vengeance. He mercilessly tyrannizes the servants, his "physician" (Jon), and his "seneschal" (Karl). When the servants are so caught up in the game that they no longer question the authenticity of their new despot, and when Jau tries to have his ugly "wife" (Schluck) poisoned and replaced by Adeluz, the situation becomes desperate. A sleeping potion eases him back into his former identity and he is allowed to awaken in his old clothing in front of the castle where he had been abducted. Although not convinced that he isn't *also* a prince, he quickly resumes his old habits and sets out for a nearby tavern where he intends to sit with the "simple people" and be very cordial, "very common" (1:1110).

The clash of two contrasting social spheres expressed in the plot is faithfully reflected in the form of *Schluck und Jau* and is a principal source of the play's humor. Interspersed with high-minded philosophical musing in iambic pentameter, lyrical inserts, and snatches of folksong, are Jau's earthy comic oaths, mispronunciations of the elegant court vocabulary, and drastic references to bodily functions; e.g., "I've shit in silk diapers as long I can remember" (1:1041). Again each character speaks an unmistakably unique language which, within the space of a few random lines, conveys something of his or her temperament, sincerity, and vulnerability.

In spite of its orchestrated dissonances, the play exudes a sense of artistic unity and harmony. This is partly the result of the "wheel of fortune" plot in which Schluck and Jau are returned to their starting point at the end of the action, but also to a carefully balanced symmetry of characterization. The six main characters all function in pairs; i.e., Schluck and Jau, Jon and Karl, and Sidselill and Adeluz. In each of these pairs one character is subordinated to the other (although which to which is not always as clear as it my appear at first glance!); while one (Schluck, Jon, and Sedselill) is less aggressive and more aesthetically oriented than his or her more practical and energetic counterpart (Jau,

Karl, and Adeluz). One of the more striking ways in which Hauptmann distinguishes between his "Apollonians" and "Dionysians" is in reference to their attitude toward animals. Jon, the aesthete, offended more by the unsightly appearance of the drunken peasants than by their trespassing, sees nature through a romantic haze. His interest is in the beauty of the hunt, and he adheres to its stylized rules. Karl, on the other hand, shares with Jau a barely suppressed and sadistic blood lust. Unlike his fastidious companion, he makes no distinction between noble game and helpless birds, slaughtering wild boar and innocent magpies with equal élan (1:1017). Like Jau, who threatens to drown everyone "like young cats" (1:1092), and who, to everyone's surprise, quickly but clumsily subdues a cantankerous horse (1:1049), he is less interested in style than substance and shows a tendency toward the same crude language; as when he swears "by the tits of my mare . . . " (1:1020) or sees himself as "a free falcon, not a tame one" (1:1060) and rejects the barony Jon offers him because of the responsibilities it would entail.

As usual with Hauptmann, one must be cautious about interpreting differing character traits in terms of moral absolutes. Sidselill's pleasure in the "long, soft, delicate little hairs" (1:1026) of a freshly killed fox is no less reprehensible, for example, than a magpie hunt. Aesthetic overrefinement and sadistic enjoyment are two sides of the same epicurean coin.

Still, to understand a character, while it may provide a basis for forgiving him, is insufficient to inspire love. The one figure in which we sense Hauptmann's unalloyed affection is Schluck. Totally without guile, he is especially vulnerable because he lacks the aggressive instincts revealed in the language of his persecutors. Not an aesthete but an artist who credits his gifts to God (1:1054–55), he keeps both feet firmly planted in reality, and his work—whether it be a somewhat flat-chested paper silhouette of Sidselill or an impossible female impersonation—reflects his best effort. The fact that he is also a poor schlemiel whose troubles lead him to seek solace in alcohol only enhances his humanity.

What has been said about the characters and suggested by the elements of downright cruelty (e.g., the abuse of poor Schluck) which show through even the most abbreviated plot outline, raises the suspicion that we are dealing with more than the innocent little comedy suggested by the subtitle. On later reflection Hauptmann himself came to speak of the play as a tragicomedy,[31] and a quick look at the work's themes confirms the correctness of this designation. At least four interrelated subjects keep recurring again and again: an almost constant awareness of death and the transitoriness of life; dreams; boredom; and the not-so-innocent games people play with, and on, each other. As Nehring has convincingly demonstrated, these themes and especially the characters of Jon, Karl, and Sidselill place Hauptmann's work in surprisingly close proximity to the Viennese Impressionists Hugo von Hofmannsthal and Arthur Schnitzler—who were known to the author personally by the time he wrote *Schluck and Jau* and whose works he had recently seen on the stage.[32]

Certainly the most basic theme, and the one from which the others derive, is the constant preoccupation with the transitoriness of life. Even Jau is aware that "we all gotta die" (1:1095) and characteristically exploits the argument in an attempt to seduce Adeluz. Jon says essentially the same thing in his own more effete language: "In the end blooms the precipice; blooms the night" (1:1061), and Karl sees the whole charade with Jau as "an illustration . . . of the transitoriness of earthly happiness!" (1:1105). Although its setting may seem timeless, the play reflects the very personal crises of its author and the crisis of faith typical of his generation. The materialist philosophers and Friedrich Nietzsche had undermined the concept of a benevolent God and a life after death; and the initially optimistic euphoria of the Naturalists, who sought solace in the belief that, at least in his earthly existence, man had some measure of control over his destiny, had faded. At best, life was incomprehensible; at worst, meaningless. In either case the result was that *tedium vitae* already expressed in Shakespeare's *Hamlet* and Goethe's *Werther*. Without a hierarchy of human activities, any and all actions are equally insignificant and life becomes a creeping fever of boredom. The behavior of the various characters in *Schluck und Jau* represents their desperate attempt to dilute this boredom as much as possible and to salvage what they can. Thus Jon, for example—like the Viennese Impressionists and Stefan George—seeks a substitute for metaphysical security in a cult of aestheticism, while Karl (and here one is reminded of Hauptmann's own sybaritic tendencies) concentrates on the more tangibly physical pleasures and distractions. The danger of such inherently selfish behavior is that it neglects and tramples on the rights and feelings of others.

A further consequence of this modern outlook is a heightened sense of uncertainty, and (even before the popularization of Albert Einstein and Sigmund Freud) Hauptmann entertained the very unnaturalistic notion of the insubstantiality of so-called "reality." The old and ambiguous concept of life being only a dream, exemplified in Jau's experience, is a staple of German Baroque thought. For the seventeenth century, however, it has religious overtones. Life is a dream in contrast to the real life after death which comes as a reward for adhering to the "rules of the game"; i.e., to religious precepts. Without the belief in a "real" life to follow, actions become indifferent, the game becomes chaotic, and the roles played have no meaning beyond the moment. Paradoxically, the less sensitive and thoughtful characters (Jau rather than Schluck) tend to be the better players since they slip into their roles so easily and completely. Captives of their id, they play their roles with such vehemence that their obsessions are mistaken for truth. Thus Hauptmann's drama is not so much about the exploitation of one class by another, as about the exploitation of human beings by human beings. Schlau, his willingness and compassion notwithstanding, is subjugated by Jau *before* the appearance of the nobles.

A still more suspect political aspect of the play lies in the dangerously contagious forces such unhealthy role-playing can unleash among those who live by instinct rather than reason. When Jon's own servant brushes him aside in order to serve Jau ("get out of the way—I'm doing my duty"), the prince is justified in concluding: "I'm dethroned" (1:1089). At this point the play becomes an object lesson on the power of obsessive role-playing; a lesson which was to be printed more indelibly on history by such consummate "actors" as Hermann Goering and Adolf Hitler.

In concluding this discussion it may be appropriate to suggest one more possible source of Hauptmann's inspiration; one which can be safely mentioned in regard to a number of his works: Georg Büchner. Without wishing to quarrel with the parallels Wolfgang Nehring establishes to Viennese Impressionism, it should be pointed out that Büchner treats death, boredom, aestheticism, and role-playing—in a manner very reminiscent of Hauptmann—in *his* serious "comedy" *Leonce und Lena*. The politically sinister nature of obsessive "actors" had already been explored in the role of Robespierre in his *Dantons Tod* [The Death of Danton].

Chapter Six
Folklore and Symbolism
Die versunkene Glocke

The failure of his tragedy *Florian Geyer* (1896) when it first appeared was a disturbing experience for Hauptmann since it seemed to signal an abrupt loss of rapport with his audience. Apparently meant as a tour-de-force application of the principles of Naturalism to the sixteenth-century Peasants' War, it describes Geyer's unsuccessful efforts to mediate between the warring factions. And, although it manages to raise the theme of petty discord to an almost quintessential flaw of the German national character, Hauptmann's ambitious attempt at re-creating the archaic language of the era, in a drama with more than sixty-five speaking roles, is enough to try the patience of any but the most dedicated audience.

The work's failure was exacerbated by a rapidly changing zeitgeist. Writing about it, the author expressed his puzzled concern in the words: "German national feeling is like a cracked bell; I struck it with my hammer but it didn't resound."[1] Four or five years earlier the drama might well have been successful. In the meantime, however, the fashion in serious literature (a fashion accelerated by the author's own *Hannele*) had begun to turn from "democratic radicalism and patriotism . . . to private experiences and non-realistic forms."[2] Sensing his mistakes, Hauptmann found it expedient to capitulate to tendencies visible in his earlier work but kept in check by the requirements of Naturalism: i.e., an affinity for the tastes of the upper middle class and a predilection for more direct personal confession. The result, *Die versunkene Glocke: Ein deutsches Märchendrama* [The Sunken Bell: A German Fairy Tale Drama], written and produced in 1896, provided the assurance he craved that he had not lost control. In spite of the strong reservations of a number of critics—not to mention Hauptmann's own uneasiness about its artistic merit—this work soon became his greatest popular and international success.[3]

In order to better understand *Die versunkene Glocke*—as well as a number of other works written during the decade between 1894 and 1904, it is useful to review briefly the more salient facts of Hauptmann's tumultuous life during that period. If read with caution against the background of biographical information available from other sources, the author's *Buch der Leidenschaft* [Book of Passion], begun in 1905 but not completed until 1929, provides an interesting outline. This roman à clef in diary form (Hauptmann spoke of it as his *Wahrheit und Dichtung* [Truth and Fiction] in contrast to the priority implied by Goethe's *Dichtung und Wahrheit*)[4] is a subjective account of the difficult marital problems that preoccupied him during this time. The very intensity of this preoccupation, combined with the author's reticence in exposing his life to public scrutiny, weakens the work both as truth and fiction. Because Titus, the hero, is not identified as the celebrated author his creator had by now become, he remains a somewhat nebulous character, defined mainly by his vacillation between two women. He leaves the impression of a man almost incapacitated by indecision and emotion; not, as in the case of his real-life counterpart, of one apparently able to transmute a difficult time of suffering into perhaps the most productive decade of a long, fruitful life.

Although the marriage of Gerhart and Marie Hauptmann seems to have been insecure from the beginning, the most severe crisis dates from November 14, 1893. It was on this date, the evening of the premiere of *Hannele,* that the poet became passionately attached to the young violinist and actress, Margarethe Marschalk, whom he had known since 1889 when she was only fourteen. Something of a tomboy who shared his interests in music, art, and sports, she seemed a complete antipode to his wife Marie, a nervous, frequently worried and depressed homebody who couldn't feel at ease with her husband's more extravagant lifestyle. *Buch der Leidenschaft* chronicles the gradual breakup of the marriage; it ended in divorce and Gerhart's marriage to Margarethe in 1904. In the novel the hero is obviously Gerhart; Melitta is Marie, and Anja is Margarethe. The reasons for the protracted nature of the dissolution are, as one might expect, portrayed rather one-sidedly from the hero's point of view. Marie, who had supported Gerhart financially until his breakthrough in 1889, and had borne him three sons, felt a proprietary interest in his success and was hurt and confused by what she saw as a physical attraction for a teen-age girl. Gerhart, conscious of his guilt, was led to establish two expensive households and, in accordance with his notions about polygamy, attempted to persuade his wife to enter into a *marriage à trois* with him and Margarethe—an idea for which she could muster no enthusiasm (Cf. 7:242–43, 246).

Among the more interesting episodes of the *Buch der Leidenschaft* for American readers is the one in which Melitta flees to the United States with her two children (the three of reality must have seemed *too* damning!) as Käthe had threatened to do under similar circumstances in *Einsame Menschen*. Hauptmann/Titus, in an attack of familial concern over the dangers of an ocean voyage, immediately followed her. Here, at the home of his friend Alfred Ploetz (alias Rauscher), who had emigrated to Meriden, Connecticut, he worked on *Der Mutter Fluch* [The Mother's Curse], an early version of *Die versunkene Glocke*.[5] He also became reconciled—at least temporarily—with his wife and family.

Hauptmann's trip in 1894 took place under circumstances little conducive to an appreciation of the new environment. In addition to his marital problems there were frustrations relating to a scheduled performance of *Hannele* in New York City. An impresario speculating on a mild scandal to increase ticket sales had cast an underage girl in the role of Hannele. The puritanical reaction of the authorities in forbidding the girl's appearance, as well as the negative attitude of the audience, which finally got to see the play with an actress who had too obviously reached her majority, did little to make the German author feel at home. The result was that, while there were aspects of America, such as its youthful vitality, that appealed to him and caused him to consider emigration, other conditions, including the frightening convolutions of modern civilization in New York, persuaded him to return to Germany with his wife and children.[6]

Back in Europe, the confusions and tribulations of Gerhart/Titus continued and were heightened by a number of events which can only be mentioned here in passing. The marital problem proved impervious to solution, and in 1902 he and Margarethe/Anja moved into the expensive mansion he built on the Wiesenstein mountain in the Riesengebirge—shortly after she had presented him with a son, Benvenuto. There were other problems as well. He was in ill-health much of the time; his brother Georg (Marcus in the novel), a failed businessman, died in 1899, and the enmity of Carl (Julius) became more intense. The fact that Carl, who had grown up thinking himself superior to his younger brother, enjoyed a considerably less spectacular literary reputation caused much bitterness and culminated in a violent scene at a family reunion during the Christmas season of 1897. *Buch der Leidenschaft* conveys a sense of this rivalry, particularly in an episode in which Titus reacts with rage over the lines beginning "Heinrich, der Wagen bricht" ("Henry, the wagon is breaking") which Julius has quoted to him from the Grimms' familiar fairy tale "The Frog King" (7:182–85). Rather obviously, the brother has touched a raw (and perhaps Freudian) nerve since Titus complains of feeling helpless and impotent during this period, most directly, perhaps, when he admits, "I notice that in both my outer and inner life I have lost the reins," and again later: "Nothing resounds in me anymore, or just as much or as little as in a bell with cracks" (7:187, 355).

Anyone familiar with the verse drama *Die versunkene Glocke* will recognize an affinity to the mood—indeed the very imagery—of the above remarks. The work opens with a fairy-tale scene by a well and the introduction of the beautiful water sprite Rautendelein ("half child, half virgin"); the merman Nickelmann (with the "brekekekex" trademark of Aristophanes' *Frogs*); and the jealously malicious Waldschrat (an over-sexed, pipe-smoking forest creature). The latter boasts of having broken the wagon of the pious founder, Heinrich, as he was laboriously hauling his masterpiece bell up into the mountainous heights. The bell has tumbled down into a lake—a circumstance Heinrich construes as a divine censure so severe that he loses faith in his creative calling and even the will to live: "I am dying: that is good. God means well. . . . My work was bad; the bell . . . which fell down, was not made for the heights, to awaken the echo of the mountain peaks" (1:801). Roused from his depression by Rautendelein, he leaves his wife Magda and their two children to enter her magic realm and try once more to create a masterpiece. As a "pilgrim of the sun," half mortal, half divine, he competes with the gods in fashioning a bell that will eclipse all those of the mortal world. But this work too comes to naught because of the human limitations of its creator. Drawn back to the valley by his conscience, he is mocked and reviled by the valley "Christians," only to learn that his long-suffering wife has died. Once more he climbs the mountain, but the magic draught that he drinks to regain Rautendelein and his former prowess also brings him death. His dying words, "the sun . . . the sun is coming!—The night is long" (1:869), are paradigmatic for the ambiguity of the entire play.

Neither the ambiguity nor the popularity of *Die versunkene Glocke* are too surprising when we consider the universality of its contemporary appeal. In form it represents Hauptmann's greatest concession to the "inwardness" of Neoromanticism, while maintaining, simultaneously, elements of Naturalism; e.g., in the earthy dialect of the Silesian witch Wittichen. The ubiquity of its ideas is shown by the fact that, almost from the day of its appearance, it has been a fertile field for influence-hunters. With more or less justification it has been linked to Arnold Böcklin's paintings; Goethe's *Satyros* and *Faust*; Grimms' fairy tales and Silesian folklore; Ibsen's *Peer Gynt, Brand, Lady from the Sea,* and the epic poem *On the Heights*; Friedrich Fouqué's *Undine*; Eduard Mörike's *Orplid*; Richard Wagner's *Nibelungen*; various works by Nietzsche including *Zarathustra*; the verse drama *Erlinde* by Goethe's grandson Maximilian; isolated ideas from the Italian utopian philosopher Thomas Campanella; Shakespeare's *Midsummer Night's Dream;* the old Germanic gods of the *Edda*; and various other "sources" too numerous to mention. [7]

Corresponding to this multiplicity of literary and cultural reminiscences is a veritable kaleidoscope of themes which Hermann Weigand describes and summarizes as follows:

The planes of symbolic meaning, confusingly multiple, keep constantly interfering with one another. For besides being a fairy drama full of laughter and pathos, *The Sunken Bell* is a social drama of a man between two women, an individual challenging an outraged bourgeois society. It is a religious drama, a battleground between ascetic Christianity and sun-worshipping paganism. It is the tragedy of the artist who revels in divine inspiration but fails in the attempt to give embodiment to his airy visions. It is, furthermore, the tragedy of mankind as a whole; there is an irremediable flaw in man, the botched product of the evolutionary process. And it is lastly a seasonal myth, tracing the cycle from nature's awakening as heralded by the spring thunder, to the rigidity of winter blanketing the valleys with the leaden clouds that drift down from the Riesengebirge. [8]

Particularly when we consider its themes and characters we soon discover that the novelty of *Die versunkene Glocke* is more apparent than real. The motifs of the man between two women of contrasting personality, of the ineffectual "artist," and of the inadequacy of Christianity were all present in *Einsame Menschen;* and, despite a greater degree of idealization, Hauptmann still relies heavily on people close to him to serve as models for his characters. The idea that art should approximate nature, Heinrich's failure to escape the determinism of his milieu, and the attacks on conventional marriage and orthodox religion are mainstays of German Naturalism. And that the play seems to have received its special impetus from personal and artistic problems arising from the author's vacillation between Marie and Margarethe on the one hand, and the failure of *Florian Geyer* on the other, tells us more about the emotional intensity with which it was written than about the originality of its content.

Some indication of this intensity, and a hint as to how it was fueled, is found—to take just one example—in the character of the Waldschrat. In this instance, Jean Jofen seems close to the mark when she identifies the pipe-puffing, physically deformed, and envious opponent of Heinrich with Hauptmann's brother Carl.[9] What Gerhart interpreted as Carl's mockery over his implied loss of vitality in the episode of "Heinrich, der Wagen bricht" is here transformed into the active, malicious deed of the Waldschrat. Motivated by disdainful jealousy of Heinrich's accomplishement, the Waldschrat "fixes his wagon"; i.e., he destroys it and silences its precious cargo, thereby plunging its author into a state of despair and creative paralysis which inhibits his art from achieving the heights for which it is intended.

The fact that Hauptmann's play displays familiar problems and features does not mean that it was not also a new departure for him. The form, for better or for worse, indicates a growing lyrical tendency; a willingness to express private emotions more openly and freely than is consistent with Naturalism. Along with this changing artistic signature there is an increased fascination with the power of Eros. And, in spite of its author's periodic return visits to Naturalism—which most critics consider Hauptmann's most congenial mode—*Die versunkene Glocke* helped establish tendencies and directions that accompanied him the rest of his life.

Und Pippa Tanzt!

According to a popular anecdote, Hauptmann was asked after the premiere of *Und Pippa tanzt!* [And Pippa Dances! (1905)] what it was that he had tried to express in this drama. "If I knew that," he is said to have answered, "I wouldn't have had to write down the whole nonsense *(Quatsch)*."[10] It is useful to repeat this brusque reply before getting too deeply involved with interpretations of the play since it amounts to an admonition not to rely too heavily on a strictly rational *explication de texte*. As the subtitle *Ein Glashüttenmärchen* [A Glassworks Fairy Tale] implies, and Hauptmann's description of the play as a *"mysterium* in a small frame"[11] tends to confirm, we should not expect tidy, precise answers to simple, direct questions. The author, as some remarks he made in 1932 indicate, saw his work as a "quest" drama, "a symboliza- tion of inward searching [in which] the outer plot is only a pretext. But not only in this fairy tale, but also in my realistic dramas the story- line—or the episodes—hardly play a role. My truth seekers are distin- guished by the fact that I only show their search but never the truth. And how could I, since I haven't yet found it myself!"[12]

The setting of "this fairy tale" is the Riesengebirge of Silesia during midwinter, and, although it isn't expressly stated, the time appears to be contemporaneous with the period of its creation. The first act parti- cularly, which takes place in a disreputable tavern frequented by glassworkers, provides a masterful example of Hauptmann's stagecraft, in that the action is carefully orchestrated on several levels simultane- ously. Upstage we are introduced to the director of the glassworks, a vain, modish and superficial man whose insensitivity is immediately established by the fact that he has completely exhausted his fine mare by a two-hour forced ride through deep snow for a trout dinner at the tavern. Further to the rear a group of men is noisily playing cards. Of these the most prominent is an Italian named Tagliazoni. He is a suspect, dangerous-looking individual but a virtuoso artisan who has brought the delicate art of Venetian glass manufacture—and his equally delicate and ethereal young daughter Pippa—to the Riesengebirge. The Director wants to enliven things. He has been dreaming about the mysterious girl and offers a hundred *lire* to see her dance. At this point, the action is briefly interrupted by the appearance of Michel Hellriegel, a travelling apprentice, but then the dance begins, although it is initiated more by old Huhn than by the Director and his money. Huhn is an enormous, primitive man with a threaten- ing, rough exterior but a sensitive soul. He too creates beautiful glass objects and dreams of Pippa. Slowly, clumsily, and to the elemental music of an ocarina, Huhn circles and grasps for the gracefully elusive girl who half entices, half rejects him. Just as the dance reaches a frenzied highpoint there is a violent commotion from the card table. Tagliazoni has used the diversion of his daughter's dance to cheat his partners. The Italian draws his knife but is pursued out into the snowy desolation. A scream signals his murder. Cowering in fear, Pippa is seized and then carried off (by now unconscious) by Huhn.

The second act takes place in Huhn's crude hut to which he has taken Pippa. Awakened from her unconsciousness by a sip of brandy, she tries to flee the old man but he restrains her and tries to calm her by bringing blankets and goat's milk. Outside a blizzard rages. Suddenly there is a knock on the window, and a voice is heard asking for refuge. Huhn, who thinks someone has come to steal his prize, arms himself with a cudgel and leaves the hut while the exhausted Pippa again drops off to sleep. At this point, Hellriegel enters, plays a few notes on the ocarina, and watches Pippa as she rises somnambulistically and begins to dance. When she comes out of her trance, she beseeches him to rescue her from Huhn, and he immediately promises to stay with her always and to take her with him on his wanderings. From outside we again hear a scream, but this one sounds like the celebration of a forest god; drawn out and powerful, it consists of the single mysterious word "Jumalai," which Michel interprets to mean "joy for all."

Act III takes place high in the mountains in the comfortable, airy home of Wann, a wise, humane, and highly civilized old man who lives alone with his mute servant Jonathan. The two are visited by the Director (briefly), by Huhn, who hides behind the oven and is not immediately noticed, and by Hellriegel and Pippa who, totally exhausted, are saved at the last minute from freezing to death. Using a small model of a gondola and the sound Pippa produces by rubbing her moistened finger on the edge of a wine glass, Wann fulfills Hellriegel's romantic longing for a trip to Venice by hypnotically transporting him there. Upon awakening from the trance, the latter recalls that Huhn is pursuing them, and gets Wann to promise to protect Pippa from the giant before going off to bed. Having also shown Pippa to her room, Wann returns and is suddenly confronted by Huhn. There is a struggle during which Wann wrestles with his opponent and prevents him from following Pippa. The act closes with another frightful cry from Huhn who collapses, as though dying, in Wann's arms.

As the curtain rises on the final act, the audience is surprised to find Huhn still alive. Wann sends Hellriegel out for a bucket of snow to place on the old man's heart to help revive him. When the youth returns, however, he has changed; he has seen the ice-demons and has lost his sight. Huhn too struggles with internal demons but gradually regains his strength, and when Pippa succumbs to the temptation to dance like a glowing spark to the music of Hellriegel's ocarina, he is strong enough to beat out the rhythm with his fists. Catching sight of Wann, however, he suddenly crushes one of the latter's beautiful Venetian glasses in his fist. As the pieces fall to the floor, Pippa collapses and dies. Once more we hear Huhn's triumphant scream of "Jumalai" and then he too expires. Hellriegel, of course, no longer sees any of this. Encouraging his fantasy, Wann pretends to marry him to Pippa, presses his staff into his hand, and sends the happily giggling youth out into the bright winter sunlight. The music of the ocarina slowly fades in the distance as Wann painfully contemplates the tiny gondola from Pippa's homeland.

Und Pippa tanzt! represents the congruence of a number of interests and passions that preoccupied Hauptmann at the turn of the century and (in some cases) until much later. At the risk of oversimplification we can isolate the more important ingredients of this drama as a longstanding interest in Silesian folklore; a German preoccupation with Italy as an antipode to the colder (climatic and emotional) atmosphere of the North which enjoyed a resurgence in the early twentieth-century *Venedigdichtung* of Hugo von Hofmannsthal, Thomas Mann, and Rainer Maria Rilke; and the short-lived but intense relationship to a young actress who provided the creative spark which fused these elements into a work of art.

Since 1897 Hauptmann had been preoccupied with the legends of the Riesengebirge, and the first fruits of this study were expressed in the dramatic fragment *Kynast*. Among the most important of these legends are the *Venedigersagen* ("legends about Venetians") concerning the so-called *Walen*, (i.e., *Welsche* = "strangers"), those mysterious fortune-seekers, accredited by the local populace with magical powers and identified culturally with the Venetian glass industry.[13] By 1898 he had conceived the idea of a dramatic trilogy, *Walenzauber* [Walen Magic] which contained the seeds not only of *Pippa* but of a number of works destined to remain fragmentary although he kept returning to them, over a period of many years: the drama *Galahad,* the terza rima epic *Der große Traum* [The Great Dream], the verse drama *Der Dom* [The Cathedral], and the ambitious novel *Der neue Christophorus* [The

New Christophorus]. The most direct precursor of the *Pippa* drama, however, is the draft of a novel, *Der Venezianer* [The Venetian], begun in 1903 and containing prefigurations of Pippa, Tagliazoni, Huhn, Wann, and the Director as well as various plot similarities.[14]

The personal element that served to transmute these materials into *Pippa* entered Hauptmann's life in the form of a humiliating passion for a golden-haired seventeen-year-old actress, Ida Orloff (1889–1945), after whom he modelled his title character and who played that role in the premiere of the play. Scarcely a year had passed after one erotic entanglement had been solved by the divorce of Marie and his marriage to Margarethe when the forty-three-year-old playwright again found himself hopelessly infatuated by the charms of this "Lolita" who, judging from the third part of *Das Buch der Leidenschaft* (published in 1966 under the title *Neue Leidenschaft* [New Passion]), took pleasure in manipulating and tormenting her famous lover. And, although this episode was short-lived—lasting only about a year—its intensity was such that it too cast its spell over Hauptmann's future work for a long time to come.[15]

With this background in mind, a closer examination of *Pippa* itself becomes more profitable. As even a plot summary suggests, the drama offers a careful balance of realistic and romantic elements. Typically, Hauptmann was familiar with the locales he described. He had had a firsthand look at the glass industry of the Riesengebirge in 1890, and his descriptions of Venice reflect a visit to that city in 1897. Furthermore, and despite the play's tendency to become increasingly symbolic as it progresses, he took pains to provide realistic explanations for everything that happens. Thus the magic mirror with which the *Walen* see over great distances has its counterpart in Wann's telescope, and their alleged ability to fly is represented by Hellriegel's hypnotic "trip" to Venice. Yet in spite of such seeming pedantry—indeed in part because of it—Hauptmann succeeds in imparting to his audience a sense of the elusive transparency of reality. At times he does so directly, as when he has Wann draw a parallel between the limited perceptivity of a ladybug and the limitations of our own sense organs for a full comprehension of our universe (2:296). Sometimes, as in Hellriegel's eccentric report to Pippa that her father had died—and the lack of sadness with which she accepts the news—he approaches the manner of the fairy tale. To weaken our hold on palpable reality even further he relies heavily on contrast and nonverbal communication: gesture, dance, and music. A good example of this is the lush ritualistic atmosphere he achieves in the first act through the juxtaposition of Pippa's dance (symbolizing pursuit and capture) and the berserk pursuit and murder of Tagliazoni—a scene all the more effective because of its setting in the realistic environs of the tavern.

In a similar vein there is something archetypal about the characters of the play. With the exception of the Director (whose function seems to be to provide banal contrast for the others), the main characters all seem to owe something to figures and types deeply embedded in German culture. Pippa's dancing and vulnerability, for example, are reminiscent of Goethe's Mignon; Hellriegel epitomizes the Romanticism of Joseph von Eichendorff; Huhn is a close relative of the local mountain spirit Rübezahl; and the wise old truth-seeker Wann is identified with the legendary *Walen* mentioned above. On another level, the central male characters all represent different, basic modalities of existence—of their author in particular and of mankind in general. Their differences (i.e., the ebullient mysticism of Hellriegel; the Dionysian vitality of Huhn; the distilled intellectual clarity of Wann, even the cheerless conviviality of the Director) notwithstanding, all have Eros, a love directed toward self-realization, in common. Even in the coldly barren atmosphere of the twentieth century, in which instinctive artistry is in danger of being supplanted by purely commercial considerations, all are fatefully attracted to Pippa, the last remaining spark from a warmer, more elemental life.[16]

If, at the conclusion of a discussion of a play whose strength is its elusiveness, questions about its "meaning" are not to be totally avoided, the final scenes of the third and fourth acts deserve a closer look. In the titanic wrestling match between the Apollonian and Dionysian forces, embodied in Wann and Huhn respectively, Hauptmann reverts to the Nietzschean dichotomy that infused so much of the literature of the day. At first, in Wann's apparent victory, light, clarity, and civilization seem to triumph over darkness, instinct, and chaos. In the end, however, it is the Dionysian forces that claim their due. Huhn, Pippa's least likely suitor, succeeds in "capturing" her and taking her with him into the larger reality of death.

Chapter Seven
Masterpieces of Realism

Fuhrmann Henschel

At first glance *Fuhrmann Henschel* [Drayman Henschel] seems a throw-back to the Naturalistic family dramas with which Hauptmann had established his reputation. Having originally written it in dialect during 1897–98, the author was forced to compromise his artistic vision (as he had done for *Die Weber*) by translating the work into a language that retained its Silesian flavor but was more easily comprehensible to non-Silesians. In reverting to the dialect of his childhood he also returned to the memories so intimately associated with it: his father's faltering hotel business; the less genteel atmosphere in the lower level of the hotel which had been leased to drayman Krause and to an ex-actor turned barkeep, and rumors about the second marriage of his grandfather to a servant girl who mistreated the illegitimate child she brought into the marriage.[1]

All five acts take place in the inn *Zum grauen Schwan* (The Gray Swan) of a Silesian spa during the eighteen sixties. The first act sets the stage for the inexorable tragedy which follows. The seriously ill wife of Henschel, although seemingly aware that her end is near, is concerned about a possible relationship between her husband and the servant girl Hanne Schäl—in spite of his protestations to the contrary and Hanne's flirtations with the coachman Franz. Henschel, a prosperous, proud, and robust man in the prime of life, finally gives in to her entreaties and promises that, if she should die, he will not marry Hanne.

By the time the second act opens several months later Mrs. Henschel has indeed died and Hanne has begun a campaign to usurp her place. By claiming that her reputation is at stake if she remains under the same roof with a widower, and threatening to leave, she puts pressure on Henschel to marry her. At first he resists, but a combination of circumstances including his need for someone to tend his sickly little daughter Gustl, the advice of Siebenhaar, the well-meaning but somewhat ineffectual owner of the hotel, and—as one gathers between the lines—the voluptuous sensuality of Hanne, weakens his resolve.

By the third act Hanne and Henschel are married and the former maid shows her true nature. Domineering, cruel, and ambitious, she repays her husband's kindness by betraying him with a young fop of a waiter named George. In the meantime Gustl has also died, and when Henschel brings Hanne's illegitimate child Bertha into the household (Hanne's father, being as irresponsible as she is, has criminally neglected the little girl), she flies into a rage and threatens to leave if he tells people she is the mother—rather redundantly since, as Henschel points out, everyone knows it anyway.

The fourth act shifts from the Henschel household to the bar of the ex-actor Wermelskirch where a dispute breaks out between Henschel and his former employee Haufe, an older man who has been dismissed because Hanne cold-heartedly maintains that he is worn out and no longer an efficient worker. The groom Walther, a brother of Henschel's first wife, intercedes. Pointing out that Henschel has changed for the worse under Hanne's influence, he insinuates that the latter may have been responsible for the death of both his sister and little Gustl, and ends by revealing to the drayman what everyone knows: that his wife is openly betraying him. Called to account, Hanne denies the accusation but runs from the room. The worst having become clear to him, Henschel, with a rattling noise in his throat, drops his head on the table and collapses.

As the final act opens, Henschel is only a shadow of his former self, and even Hanne seems awed by his decline. Plagued by insomnia and visions of his first wife, he is tortured by his broken promise. Siebenhaar and Wermelskirch try to console and distract him but to no avail, and he goes off into his room with the remark that "everything will look different tomorrow" (1:1003). Hanne, concerned, calls to him but there is no answer. When Siebenhaar enters the room to find out what has happened, he immediately returns, deathly pale, and with little Bertha on his arm. Henschel has killed himself.

Highly praised by such contemporaries as Thomas Mann, Maxim Gorki, and the popular dialect author Hermann Stehr,[2] *Henschel* brought its author a second Grillparzer Prize in 1899 (the first was for *Hannele,* three years earlier) and is recognized to this day as one of his best and most characteristic works.

Like *Bahnwärter Thiel,* albeit in quieter, less melodramatic tones, it deals with a central problem we have encountered before and we shall continue to encounter: the problematic, guilt-ridden relationship between a man and two very different women. And, although it will not do to equate Thiel and Henschel, or Lene and Hanne—Henschel's instincts are less obvious than Thiel's and Hanne's hold on him is less overtly demonic—both heroes fall victim to a crisis of conscience and a rampant, destructive femininity. By nature, intellect, profession, and social status Henschel starts out higher than Thiel (and falls deeper) but the two share a closeness to nature, a compassion for children, and a tendency to repress uncomfortable facts and feelings until they explode in violence. Finally, both men undergo progressive religious crises and psychological deterioration, causing them to see visions of their former wives and, when suffering exceeds their powers of endurance, both find a strange, resigned equanimity: Thiel in his madness and Henschel just before he commits suicide.

While nobody would deny that *Fuhrmann Henschel* is firmly anchored in a particular social milieu (a self-evident requirement for a Naturalist work), one must be cautious about overstressing this feature. True, there seem to be traces of the popular "marriage lie" theme in the drama, and Hanne's social climb appears to claim its victims, Hauffe, for example. However, the work is much too complex and ambiguous to permit a neat separation into moral, psychological, and social motivations. The marriage is more than a cold business arrangement, and Hanne's treatment of Hauffe reveals a sadistic element no more attributable to purely economic factors than her cruelty toward her own child. And to lament the fact that Hauptmann failed to motivate Henschel's suicide in terms of an economic setback[3] is to misconstrue his intentions. There is an archetypal substratum to the play that Thomas Mann recognized when he described it as an "Attic tragedy in contemporary realistic form."[4] Henschel is a latter-day Job who conceives his situation in terms of fate and who achieves peace through suffering in the sight of an inscrutable God.[5]

In keeping with the increased "interiorization" of the action, as compared with the early *Vor Sonnenaufgang,* for example, are the subtle changes in form. Although outwardly Naturalistic in such aspects as the use of dialect and extensive stage directions, the overall structure is tauter. The temptation to engage in displays of linguistic virtuosity for their own sake has been curtailed; shock effects and sentimentality have been largely eliminated, and distracting motifs which do not contribute to the direct line of action are kept in check. The result is a mature, powerful, and timeless drama.

Michael Kramer

Written in 1900 and performed in December of that year, *Michael Kramer,* and particularly its last act, antagonized some spectators and critics while enchanting many others.[6] Especially for a number of fellow artists, its impression was deep and lasting. "How I loved that last act, with Arnold Kramer's coffin in the glow of candles, when death has elevated and transfigured this ugly man,"[7] Thomas Mann was to confess later, while for the poet Rainer Maria Rilke the work had the force of a mystical revelation. Not only did he see it as "Hauptmann's greatest accomplishment so far," but also in a letter to the author he begged permission to dedicate his own *Buch der Bilder* [Book of Images] to him "in order to somehow sum up my appreciation for *Michael Kramer* and to establish a connection with the best and dearest which the last years have given me."[8] For James Joyce, the encounter was, if anything, even more fruitful. Having learned German mainly to read Hauptmann, he continued to hold him in high esteem throughout his life. As early as 1901, as a young student, he practiced his sparse German by translating *Michael Kramer* into English; with the result that he practically memorized the play. It is not too farfetched to imagine that he may have learned something about his famous "epiphanies" from this study, and there is little doubt that he was strongly influenced by *Michael Kramer* in works such as "The Dead" (from *Dubliners*) and *Ulysses.*[9]

The action of the tragedy that aroused such interest in Rilke, Mann, and Joyce is set in a turn-of-the-century Prussian provincial capital. It shifts from Michael Kramer's apartment in the first act, to his atelier in the second, to a not very reputable restaurant in the third, and back once more to the atelier for the conclusion in the fourth. The titular hero is physically present only in Acts II and IV—in the atelier which he equates with his very existence, but his presence is strongly felt throughout the play in the characters whose lives he has dominated. These include Michaline, a somewhat masculine, old-maidish daughter who is also an artist and, as her name suggests, has been raised pretty much in his own image; her brother Arnold, a talented but physically unattractive and troubled, rebellious son whom he has rejected for his refusal to live up to the potential of his artistic genius; and Lachmann, a former student who was once (and perhaps still is) emotionally attached to Michaline but married instead a silly, shallow woman and has likewise failed to fulfill his mentor's expectations.

The strongest conflict is that between father and son. Instead of subscribing to his father's work ethic, i.e., striving diligently to perfect what Michael considers his extravagance of God-given talent, Arnold wastes his time in fruitless infatuation with a pretty but unworthy waitress, Liese Bänsch. Night after night he sits in her father's restaurant, humiliated by her rejection and the taunts of a group of Philistines, steady customers upon whom he takes revenge in the caricatures he draws of them. Finally, on the very evening when Michaline and Lachmann happen to visit the same restaurant, the pain becomes too great. Provoked once more, Arnold takes out a revolver, has it wrenched from his grip, dashes out the door past his shocked sister, and drowns himself.

The last act belongs, in large degree, to Michael Kramer. In a rambling panegyric addressed mainly to himself and to the audience he speaks of love, art, and death.

An act-by-act summary of this sparse plot is as inadequate as the linear, verbal description of a musical composition would be. As Victor Wittkowski wrote to Hauptmann in 1935, the play is "a tragic symphony, a music heavy with fate."[10] It exemplifies the limited usefulness of such labels as "Naturalism" or "Neoromanticism" when applied to the author's best work while paradoxically demonstrating the value of the self-imposed formal restraints that an apprenticeship to Naturalist practice could inculcate. Like its hero—although certainly not as one-sidedly—the play reveals a deep commitment to craftsmanship and the hard work implicit in an almost superhuman attention to detail. Each of the characters, no matter how minor, speaks a personalized language which reveals something of the user's psyche and attitudes. The names are distinctively Silesian; act endings are carefully orchestrated and contribute to the organic unity of the work; the stage directions carefully prime the actors with psychological as well as physical "material" for their roles; and a profound wisdom concerning heredity and psychology unobtrusively reveals itself in the service of a realistic depiction of human relationships.[11]

Craftsmanship and talent notwithstanding, part of the explanation for Hauptmann's success is that, like many modern authors, he gets along quite well with variations on a few basic themes (which he can hone to ever greater perfection in succeeding works) and with a relatively small number of character types constituting varying blends of imagined features and traits freely borrowed from real people: himself, his family, and those he knew intimately. Thus *Michael Kramer* is not only the tragedy of an artist but a family tragedy like *Das Friedensfest* as well. As happens in that drama, it depicts an older couple with little understanding for each other or their offspring who, more from ignorance and inherent predisposition than malice, handicap the lives of their children. Like such disparate characters as Wilhelm Scholz, Johannes Vockerat, or the bellfounder Heinrich, Michael, Michalaline, and Arnold Kramer are flawed artists whose work falls short of their aspirations. And like *Die Weber* or *Hannele,* but less ambiguously so, the play ends on a metaphysical note in which suffering leads to illumination.

To anyone familiar with the details of Hauptmann's early life the biographical reminiscences in *Michael Kramer* are hard to overlook. Since they have been traced in some detail elsewhere[12] it will suffice here to summarize them in passing. Like Minna Scholz from *Das Friedensfest,* Mrs. Kramer seems modeled in part on the author's mother. A restless, worried complainer, she half blackmails her children by voicing a not too genuine death wish (esp. 1:1118, 1127). *Her* child—he exhibits similar characteristics in tragic form—is Arnold. Michaline, a rather masculine, cigarette-smoking (in 1900) old maid who takes after her father in temperament and *Weltbild,* reminds one of Gerhart's older sister Johanna. For Lachmann, Hauptmann claims to have been inspired by a friend from his art school days in Breslau, Hugo Ernst Schmidt, who had just died in 1899. Michael Kramer is a more complex composite, including characteristics of at least three people: Hauptmann's father, Albrecht Bräuer (a favorite teacher at the Breslau art school), and the playwright himself. Like Hauptmann senior, the elder Kramer—down to his highly polished shoes (Cf. 7:517, 1:1128)—is an obsessively neat, stiffly formal, outwardly cold individual. An almost archetypal Prussian paterfamilias from this period, he inspires fear in his badly dressed and much more overtly emotional son—a relationship similar to that between the author and his father. Like Kramer, the painter Bräuer worked for years behind closed doors on a portrait of Christ, but then, in a sense, so did Hauptmann. His extended "Jesus Studies," an outline for a drama about Christ, plus an unfinished novel about the Savior certainly parallel Kramer's tenacious struggles, and the two artists—real and fictional—share a very similar attitude toward death. The most autobiographical figure, however, is Arnold, a virtual self-portrait from one of the darkest periods of the author's youth. Like the younger Kramer, Hauptmann was no stranger to rejection and unrequited love, and during his Breslau art school days he lived a similar Bohemian life. What little money he could get his hands on "was poured on the bar of Frau Müller, or stuck into the bosom of the waitress or otherwise squandered" (7:797). Although not actually deformed physically like Arnold, his posture was bad, he considered himself ugly, and the outlandishness of his appearance, with which he tried to draw some attention to himself in compensation for his inferiority feelings, was exacerbated by a poverty so extreme that he wore the same shabby outfit winter and summer (7:797). Like Arnold, Hauptmann was accused of laziness; like him he considered suicide; and like him he dreamt of revenging himself on his tormentors through a great artistic achievement. His dramatic fragments from this period, *Frithiofs Brautwerbung* [Frithiof's Courtship], *Konradin,* and *Athalarich,* all featured "as heroes humiliated figures who, like Arnold, . . . wished to assert their power and manhood against a world of opposing forces."[13] Unlike Arnold he achieved at least some local renown with his *Germanen und Römer,* but his real salvation resulted from his relationship with Marie Thienemann—a salvation denied his unhappy fictional counterpart.

Through the medium of these intimately conceived characters *Michael Kramer* expresses ideas that in German literature were to be identified most indelibly with Thomas Mann: the artist as isolated outsider attracted to the vitality of the bourgeois world but unable to find happiness in it, and the view of art as a tightrope dance between instinct and intellect, inspiration and hard work, Dionysian and Apollonian forces. Just as Mann does in *Tonio Kröger* (1903), Hauptmann uses the then very modern technique of exteriorizing the internal struggles of his hero(es) in very different character types,[14] although, psychologist that he is, he does so somewhat less unambiguously than his younger contemporary. In *Tonio Kröger* the split is between the healthy, blonde, and blue-eyed innocents Hans Hansen and Ingeborg Holm, whom Tonio loves with unrequited passion, and the clumsy, unattractive, "sincere" Magdalena Vermehren, who, to his dismay, is attracted to him. In *Michael Kramer* the equivalents for Arnold are the pretty, empty-headed Liese Bänsch on the one hand, and the poor, "somewhat deformed" (1:1164) girl he had never noticed, but who painted because he did, and who expresses her love through an expensive floral arrangement for his funeral, on the other.

A similar dichotomy can be observed in the elder Kramer.[15] His ideal is a "healthy art," the product of a "healthy body, healthy mind, healthy life" (1:1140), and he praises Michaline for his own qualities: the industry, tenacity, and strength of character he finds totally absent in Arnold. The genius that he and Michaline lack, however, he discerns in his son. Precisely because the father's judgment is clouded and he wants his son to compensate for his own failure, Michael believes that the two components (i.e., genius and industry) found jointly in the same individual would result in an ideal artist and great works. Hauptmann himself, however, seems to subscribe to the view widely held in the nineteenth and early twentieth centuries that, in terms of physical and mental health, genius and normalcy are incompatible. With Lachmann he entertains the idea that "the strength to hold illusions is the best possession in the world" (1:1152), but like Mann's heroes he sees too deeply to avail himself of such illusionary solace as remains the preserve of the artless, practical bourgeois. For this reason it will not do to identify the author too closely with the title figure of the play; his sympathies are more with Arnold. Although Michael still persists in blaming others, rather than his own rejection, for the suicide of his son, he has by the end of the play vaguely begun to understand that a rigid ethos of work and conventional morality must be leavened with love and tolerance if it is to produce anything of lasting human value. Only after having learned this lesson, beside the body of his dead son, does he become a real artist.

To limit an interpretation of *Michael Kramer* to the "artist problem," however, would certainly do violence to Hauptmann's intentions, since his main interest is in the basic human predicament. And although the last act seems a bit too melodramatic and theatrical for present-day tastes, it is clear that the generation of Rilke, Mann, and Joyce could be deeply moved by it. Here we have Hauptmann's philosophy of suffering in perhaps its most explicit form: the belief that suffering is unavoidable and even necessary to bring out our highest potential as human beings and the intuition that "death is the gentlest form of life: the masterpiece of eternal love."[16]

Rose Bernd

"A song is its beginning; its conclusion a scream."[17] With this succinct characterization Alfred Kerr summarized the action and mood of *Rose Bernd* (1903). The drama, which "doubtless belongs . . . among Hauptmann's most significant plays"[18] is typical, in a number of ways. Like *Fasching* it owes its inception to a real event: this time the trial of a waitress accused of perjury and infanticide in which Hauptmann played an important role as a juror. Like *Die Weber* it provoked the wrath of censors (it was banned in Vienna) but gradually achieved respectability and even wide popularity (as attested to by the two film versions of 1919 and 1956).[19] Finally, like most of Hauptmann's work, it represents an amalgamation of biographical and literary materials.

The action takes place in rural Silesia, shortly after the turn of the century, and opens on a sunny Sunday morning in May. As the curtain rises, the robust young peasant girl Rose Bernd is seen stepping out of a clump of willow bushes from which Christoph Flamm, a prosperous landowner, likewise soon appears. The flushed appearance of the girl and Flamm's good humor—he bursts into a cheerful song about the joys of the hunt—makes it clear that an assignation has just taken place. During their ensuing conversation we learn that Flamm is married to a woman who has been an invalid for years and that he has availed himself of Rose's sexual favors for some time. While their enjoyment and guilt is mutual, he makes it clear that he will not consider divorcing his wife to marry her. The situation is further complicated by the fact that Rose has promised her father to marry August Keil, a sickly, pious bookbinder of unprepossessing exterior and in poor circumstances. Flamm's heated response to this revelation is interrupted by a rustling noise and, to avoid being compromised, he takes to his heels, leaving Rose behind working in a potato field. At this point "handsome" Arthur Streckmann, a married steam-engine operator and village Don Juan, appears.

He has witnessed the activity in the bushes and will be silenced not by the savings Rose offers him but only if she will yield herself to him also. When her father and August appear on the scene (they are going home from church) Streckmann teases the bookbinder about his impending marriage.

Having established his fateful constellation of forces in the first act, Hauptmann slowly but inexorably introduces circumstance after circumstance that closes the snare around his heroine.

The second act, in Flamm's home, is devoted to further character development; to a confrontation between August, father Bernd, and Flamm, and then to a long, revealing conversation between Rose and Mrs. Flamm. Since he also serves as a kind of justice of the peace, it is Flamm's distasteful duty to make the legal arrangements for the marriage he despises. Torn between her attraction for her lover and an obligation to August and her father, Rose begins to vacillate, much to the consternation of old Bernd, who leaves abruptly with August. Rose soon finds herself alone with Mrs. Flamm. The latter, a noble-minded woman whose life as an invalid has heightened her sensitivity for the suffering of others, has always been sympathetic toward Rose and accepts her almost as a daughter. Unaware of the affair with her husband, she consoles the young woman when Rose reveals that she is pregnant.

Act Three takes place on a hot August afternoon in the hay fields of the Flamm estate where August, old Bernd, and a number of workers are mowing grass. Rose appears to bring the men their food and is soon followed by Streckmann and, later, by Flamm. By now she has been sexually coerced by Streckmann and has decided to go through with the marriage to August since she desperately needs a father for her unborn child. When Streckmann—obviously somewaht intoxicated—arrives on the scene, he immediately begins to harass August and old Bernd with insinuations about Rose which they are in no position to fully understand. The tension mounts further when Rose is seen speaking to Flamm (who admits the necessity for ending their relationship) and when Streckmann, his sexual envy aroused, tries again to impose himself upon her. Beside herself, she screams at him that he has abused her ("Du hust mir Gewalt agetan!" [2:228]). The noise brings August to her defense, but in the fight which follows he loses an eye to his much stronger opponent.

Act Four opens in Flamm's house in the fall. The act of violence has resulted in a trial during which Bernd has also accused Streckmann of slandering his daughter. Since Flamm has been called as a witness, his wife has come to understand her husband's complicity and guilt. Nevertheless, she promises to stand by Rose and to help her. The latter, however, out of deep despair and excruciating shame denies every-thing—just as she had perjured herself at the trial. Even Flamm, having misconstrued her relationship to Streckmann, turns against her.

By the last act—located in Bernd's coldly austere home—Rose's mental state has deteriorated badly. August, considerably mellowed through his own suffering, offers to move with her to a different region and a new life in spite of the fact that he has come to suspect the true state of affairs. Bernd, however, not as clairvoyant, and concerned that his position as a church elder is in jeopardy, insists that the legal battle be continued to clear his daughter's name. Only when August tells him what he knows does he break down. Rose comes out of her room distraught, and to the policeman who has come to serve her a further summons she remarks: "I have strangled my child with my hands!!" (2:258). The policeman rejects the confession as feverish fantasy, but August realizes she has told the truth and the play ends with his words: "The girl . . . how she must have suffered!" (2:259).

This uncharacteristically complex plot is further complicated by difficulties of communication between different generations, sexes, and social classes, and by the fact that the decisive actions such as the "rape" of Rose by Streckmann, the trial, and the infanticide take place between acts. And while the drama is "open" and "modern" enough to tax the creative participation of even the most sensitive audience (an eye for detail and gesture, an ear for linguistic nuance and meaningful silence, and an awareness of social and psychological contexts are important prerequisites), it is also firmly anchored in German literary tradition and the personal experience of its author.

The venerable genealogy of *Rose Bernd* includes the tradition of the *Bürgerliches Trauerspiel* ("Middle-class tragedy") and the *Kindesmörderin* ("infanticide") theme.[20] Both had their origins in the eighteenth century and have a natural tendency to merge. Familiar representatives of the former include Lessing's *Emilia Galotti,* Schiller's *Kabale und Liebe* [Love and Intrigue] and Hebbel's *Maria Magdalene,* and, of the latter, Heinrich Leopold Wagner's *Kindesmörderin* and the Gretchen episode of

Goethe's *Faust I*. Comparisons with Wagner's Storm-and-Stress play and the Hebbel work are most instructive, although there is also a definite kinship between the Ophelia-like mental deterioration of Gretchen and Rose. In terms of shock value, Hauptmann's play is actually less "Naturalistic" than Wagner's as the latter depicted at least the offstage sounds of sexual coercion and had his heroine commit infanticide, with a large knitting needle, in full view of the audience.[21] The ties to *Maria Magdalene* are stronger; so strong in fact that one early critic rejected *Rose Bernd* on the grounds that it was imitative of Hebbel to the point of plagiarism.[22] Like Hauptmann, Hebbel had placed his heroine in an untenable position between male sexual egoism and a stubborn father whose love for his daughter is vitiated by a narrowly proscribed social, moral, and religious code of conduct. (The fact that Hebbel's Maria kills her *unborn* child by committing suicide is not a very substantive difference.)

Hauptmann's play, of course, is also about female sexuality. Rose is a positive version of those robust, heavy-limbed *femmes fatales* Lene Thiel and Hanne Schäl/Henschel, and, although she doesn't ruthlessly exploit it, her erotic fascination is so persuasive that it is the equivalent of a fate which leads inexorably to destructive acts. Here too there are literary precedents familiar to Hauptmann: Büchner's sexually driven Marion in *Dantons Tod* and his Marie from *Woyzeck,* to mention two of the more obvious examples.

That Hauptmann's play represents more than a skillful continuation of literary tradition is again largely due to its biographical elements. In addition to the trial mentioned previously, these include the author's own traumatic marital problems—reflected in Flamm's vacillation between his wife and a sensually attractive younger woman—and a conscious attempt to recapture the atmosphere of rural Silesia absorbed during the author's Lederose period. There is something of the acerbic piety of the Schubert family in the Bernd household. Hauptmann's uncle had owned and operated a steam-powered threshing machine of the type so closely identified with Streckmann throughout the play; and August Keil is reminiscent of the younger author himself—including the detail that Hauptmann also once feared that he had lost an eye in a fight.[23]

Perhaps because the playwright stressed so strongly his intention to return to dialect its innate dignity and to show that the lower classes too are capable of experiencing real tragedy there has been a tendency in recent interpretations to stress the drama's metaphysical aspects. These readings depict Rose as a victim of existential loneliness, gradually pushed toward nihilism by inescapable suffering but denied the enlightenment that is usually the reward for such suffering in Hauptmann's work.[24] (Actually this process of illumination is not entirely absent but it manifests itself in Keil rather than in Rose). While there is no need to deny this aspect, the very strong individualization of the characters (down to Hauptmann's boast that Rose speaks differently to the various people she meets)[25] makes it difficult for a theater audience to see them in terms of abstractions. A stronger tendency is to identify with Rose's predicament and to puzzle over its causes.

Of these the psychological element, especially as it relates to Flamm, appears to be the most personal and troubling. Although he does not appear in the tragic fifth act, Flamm, of all the main characters, is most heavily burdened with guilt. He is, after all, the father of Rose's illegitimate child but grasps at excuses to desert her. If we compare this fictional situation with Hauptmann's personal life at the time, it is tempting to see it in terms of displaced guilt. Unlike Flamm, and after a great deal of self-recrimination, the author did leave his wife to live with the mother of his illegitimate son. The fate of Rose Bernd may, therefore, have helped Hauptmann allay his sense of guilt toward Marie by reassuring him that, as opposed to his alter ego Flamm, he had behaved decently. Additional balm for his injured self-esteem was provided by August Keil, the play's paragon of high-minded morality, with whom he could also identify.

The stages of the play's genesis suggest that Hauptmann's growing identification with Flamm parallels the increasing attractiveness of this character. In the early sketches (9:1031–61) Flamm's physical attractiveness is not stressed and he comes across as a rather brutal womanizer, who, like others in his position, habitually exploit their female employees sexually while keeping them and their families on a bare subsistence level economically. Here the illicit relationship is not enhanced by affection. The stress is on social criticism (as in the first four acts of *Die Weber*) and religion plays no role at all.

As Müller-Salget has demonstrated, this progression from specific social criticism to generalized metaphysical overtones and conclusions is by no means an isolated phenomenon in Hauptmann's work.[26]

Perhaps it indicates cowardice or a growing reluctance to offend the status quo. Perhaps, on the other hand, it represents Hauptmann's hardly unique conviction that to survive as literature a work must transcend its specific origins—whether biographical or political—and address itself to universal human problems.

Die Ratten

In contrast to that accorded to *Rose Bernd*, the critical reception of *Die Ratten* [The Rats] when it was first performed in 1911 was lukewarm. Only gradually during the intervening years (and especially since World War II) has this drama been recognized as one of the greatest accomplishments of its author. It is as if criticism needed to undergo a certain amount of historical and literary schooling in order to cope with its modernity. Expressionist drama; the work of Ibsen, of Wedekind, of Franz Kafka; the epic theater of Brecht; the modern propensity (Friedrich Dürrenmatt) for revealing tragedy through the grotesque; the collage technique of combining nondramatic forms (e.g., the detective story or the ballad) with traditional dramatic ones; a feeling for the life of Berlin during the decades *after* 1911—all this and more had to insinuate itself into our consciousness before a deeper appreciation became possible.[27]

The first impression one gets while reading this *Berliner Tragikomödie* is that of a return to an almost "classical" Naturalism. Set in a teeming, rat-infested tenement (converted from an earlier cavalry barracks) in a deteriorating neighborhood, with the noise of the gigantic city in the background, the play offers detailed stage directions which prepare us for another urban exposé à la Holz/Schlaf. This seems especially true for the more important of the two main strands of action, the one centered on Paul John, a masonry foreman, and his wife Henriette. Having lost an infant son, the couple is childless and, what with the husband out of the city on jobs for weeks at a time, Mrs. John is concerned about her marriage. Thinking herself pregnant, she has reported the glad tidings to her husband only to discover that her hopes have been premature. So as not to disappoint him—or her own strong motherly instincts—she persuades Pauline Piperkarcka, a distraught, pregnant, unmarried Polish servant girl, to sell her her unwanted child, with the intention of

passing it off as her own. For a short time after the birth the ruse seems
to work. Then the emotional Pauline has a change of heart and demands
her baby back. Mrs. John strenuously resists, reminding the girl that
just recently she had threatened to drown herself and the child. Matters
are complicated, however, by the fact that Pauline has officially recorded the birth of her son and listed Mrs. John as his foster mother.
When exposure seems inevitable, the latter substitutes the sickly infant
of a neighbor, Sidonie Knobbe (an unfortunate drug addict and woman
of ill repute), for her "own" (i.e., Pauline's) child and flees the city.
When the Knobbe child dies shortly thereafter, it seems safe for Mrs.
John to return—especially since Pauline is unsure of the identity of the
dead child. Unfortunately for Mrs. John, events have by now gathered
an irresistible momentum of their own. Mrs. Knobbe complains about
her "stolen" baby, and Bruno Mechelke, a younger brother of Mrs.
John, whom she had asked to threaten Pauline, has murdered her
instead and is a hunted man. Paul John finally learns that his supposed
fatherhood has been a deception—Selma Knobbe, Sidonie's unfortunate, harassed daughter blurts out the details—and he turns on his
wife. Mrs. John, further disturbed by a policeman who has come to take
"her" child to an orphanage, dashes into the street and kills herself by
jumping under the wheels of a horse-drawn streetcar.

Contrasting with this essentially dark and tragic strand of the plot is
a lighter, predominantly comic one which provides a certain epic
distance from the painful story of Mrs. John. The main protagonists
here are Harro Hassenreuter, a former theater director, and Erich
Spitta, a young theology student who, much to the dismay of his
theologian father, has decided to become an actor. Having fallen on lean
times, Hassenreuter is using the attic above the John quarters as a
storage place from which he rents theatrical props and costumes.

In the Hassenreuter world, too, things are rather consistently *not*
what they seem to be, but with less tragic consequences. Currying favor
from people in high places as though it were the most natural thing in
the world, the director, by the end of the play, regains his former
illustrious position as theater director in Strassburg. Along the way he
is casually unfaithful to his wife by betraying her with an actress who
specializes in "naive" roles, and to his artistic principles, not only by
accepting a student, Spitta, whose artistic ideals are diametrically

opposed to his own, but by promising the young man his daughter's hand in marriage as well. (The daughter, Walburga, knows about the affair with the actress and is not above using a little blackmail.) Spitta, a somewhat less ridiculous and more sympathetic character, gives Hauptmann the opportunity to attack several favorite targets; e.g., the highly stylized but enormously influential Weimar school of acting codified in Goethe's "infamous" rules, and the hypocrisy of orthodox religion. Unlike the John action, with which it is interwoven, the Hassenreuter/Spitta strand seems to lead effortlessly to a happy ending: Hassenreuter has maneuvered himself back into his old position, and the young lovers are engaged to be married.

Die Ratten is based on experiences the author had had a quarter century earlier (around 1885) in Berlin. At that time he had considered becoming an actor and had taken acting lessons from a man named Alexander Heßler who, like Hassenreuter, had been a director in Strassburg, eventually regained the position through influential help, and spent the intervening years renting costumes and giving lessons in a tenement building. Like Spitta, with whom Hauptmann is unmistakably identified (e.g., by his views on acting; by his lisp; and, perhaps, even by Spitta's first name, Erich [i.e., Er/ich = "he/I"]), the experience exposed the author to a great deal of urban social misery. Even at that time he pondered the motif of a servant girl who gives up and then reclaims her child, but a more personal impetus for the work may have been the loss of his own infant son in 1910.[28]

While these biographical correspondences with *Die Ratten* go a long way toward explaining Hauptmann's attraction for his materials, the problems of smoothly combining such disparate elements remained formidable. Judged in terms of the traditional concept of unity of action, there is some merit to the argument that the tragedy of Mrs. John and the comedy of Hassenreuter tend to run parallel to, rather than meshing with, each other. Disregarding for a moment the importance of atmosphere for Hauptmann—as well as the possibility of a productive tension inherent in such a contrastive technique—there is no denying that the play can be appreciated on two levels: that of social criticism, identified most explicitly with the Hassenreuter action, and another more human or even archetypal level, associated with the John plot.

The targets of Hauptmann's social criticism are, by and large, those we have encountered before and include the unhealthy influence of an oppressive state over its citizens, the destructive elements of a smugly complacent religious orthodoxy, and the hypocrisy of social institutions that are in conflict with basic human instincts. High positions are dispensed on the basis of subservience rather than ability; marriage is a covenant of convenience to be broken on the slightest provocation; and theology is a codified system of theory devoid of humanity—as when Spitta's theologian father is depicted as having cast out and driven to suicide his own daughter for allowing herself to be seduced while working in a "noble" household (2:767).

A more extraneous, idiosyncratic theme, at first glance, seems to be the running discussion between Hassenreuter and Spitta regarding the true nature of drama. Anticipating similar exercises by such authors as Brecht (*Der Messingkauf* [The Brass Purchase]) and Luigi Pirandello (*Six Characters in Search of an Author*) in which drama is made the vehicle for discussions about drama, Hauptmann seems here to be indulging a merely personal whim. On closer inspection, however, it turns out that this theme is as important as any other for understanding his dramatic intentions. On a superficial level it contributes to the characterization of Hassenreuter and Spitta. By his rigorous adherence to the dictatorial, mechanical, Goethean *Regeln für Schauspieler* ("Rules for Actors") Hassenreuter is stamped as an archconservative intent upon maintaining an outdated status quo which places style above substance and glosses over the manifold problems of a modern industrialized society with a thin veneer of elitist "culture." To the young Spitta such tendencies are anathema. Conscious of the social misery around him, he subscribes fully to the more extreme variety of Naturalist dramaturgy, a realistic acting style, and a theater devoid of Schillerian pathos devoted to expressing life as it is instead of as it should be. For him tragedy is no more the preserve of the powerful and great than of the poor and ordinary.

More important still the dramaturgical discussions also provide a key to a more profound appreciation of *Die Ratten*. Even if he had not confessed as much later,[29] Hauptmann obviously sides with the naive Spitta over the pompous Hassenreuter. Less obvious is the fact that both teacher and student represent earlier stages of his own artistic development. During his pre-Naturalist phase he still wrote with an epigonal pathos that even Hassenreuter would have relished. This phase was succeeded by his early successes (especially *Vor Sonnenaufgang*) which stressed the then-fashionable dogma of Naturalism to a point dangerously close, on occasion, to unintentional humor—a phase which corresponds roughly to that attained by Spitta. Only gradually did his views on tragedy deepen and coalesce into his concept of the *Urdrama* ("primeval drama"). While this development is too gradual to be pinpointed precisely, the year 1907, during which he was able to visit Greece, the ideal realm he had longed for since his student days, is an important landmark. His travel diary, *Griechischer Frühling* [Greek Spring (1908)], constitutes a rejection of Classical antiquity in terms of "noble simplicity and quiet grandeur," and issues into an ecstatic paean to archetypal, cultic, Dionysian tragedy. "It cannot be denied," he proclaims, "tragedy means: enmity, persecution, hatred, and love as a rage to live! Tragedy means: fear, anguish, danger, pain, torture, martyrdom, . . . malice, crime, baseness, . . . murder, bloodlust, incest, butchery. . . . To see a true tragedy would be to catch sight of Medusa's face while almost being turned into stone; it would mean to anticipate horror in a way that life secretly always holds it in readiness, even for Fortune's favorite" (7:80).[30]

In the John plot Hauptmann gives us the opportunity "to catch sight of Medusa's face." Here we have "fear, anguish, danger, pain, torture." The comic overtones in the depiction of her character notwithstanding, the cruelty of her position drives Pauline Piperkarcka to the verge of suicide and infanticide. The Knobbe child dies grotesquely of neglect during an argument over who owns it. Bruno kills Pauline almost as if in a trance. Mrs. John is driven to the edge of insanity by the exaggeration of a beautiful human emotion: motherly love. Here, among simple people, there is no dearth of "enmity, persecution, hatred, and love as a rage to live!" The fact that these events take place all around Hassenreuter and Spitta while both look on as ineffectual, largely uncomprehending spectators, not only demonstrates the inadequacy of their theories of tragedy to deal with real life; it is an indictment of them as human beings as well. Mrs. John, who has been seized, shaken, and destroyed by life, has also come much nearer to "authentic existence" than both of these intellectuals taken together.

It should be clear by now that the two plot lines are mutually supporting. The author achieves additional unity through humor, atmosphere, and the central symbol of the rats referred to in his title. As Karl S. Guthke has shown in some detail, this "most successful of Hauptmann's tragicomedies" derives its power from an inextricable blend of comic and tragic elements, not only in the plot, but within the characters as well.[31] To cite just a few examples, Hassenreuter has been playing roles for so long that, his comic "impersonations" notwithstanding, he has been bereft of any genuine identity at all. There is something both tragic and humorous in Erich Spitta's missed calling. A young man with the compassion and zeal to be an excellent pastor or social worker perversely insists on pursuing a career in play-acting. Pauline Piperkarcka's desperate situation is somehow individualized and humanized by her cruelly humorous attempts to express herself in an alien medium: the German language. Even in Frau John we detect traditionally tragicomic features; in particular the exaggeration of a virtue (in this case her mother instinct) to the point where it becomes grotesque.

This glissando between comedy and tragedy has a counterpart in the elusive atmosphere of the play that is compounded of fake past grandeur (Hassenreuter's costumes) and a brutally realistic present (Pauline's unwanted child is born amidst this theatrical junk); of ghosts (the soldier Sorgenfrei [i.e., "carefree"!] who allegedly killed himself in the attic and still haunts the place); of elements of cheap crime stories (Bruno kills Pauline under a *lilac bush*!); and much, much more. The play represents a veritable kaleidoscope of perspectives that cannot be exhausted by the central symbol of the rats—although a last quick glance at that symbol may review for us at least the direction of Hauptmann's intentions. To Hassenreuter the rats are Spitta and those like him, who are gnawing away at the roots of German idealism; to many readers and spectators the rat-infested tenements symbolize the decay of the entire Wilhelminian social structure, and, finally, if we catch Hauptmann's hint in his rodent-like description of Bruno (2:737), the rats signify those uncontrollably destructive subterranean forces "that life secretly always holds . . . in readiness, even for Fortune's favorite."

Chapter Eight
Dionysus and Christ

Although visible in such dramas as *Die Weber, Hannele,* and *Die versunkene Glocke,* Hauptmann's intensive concern with the Christian experience was largely reserved for three prose works: *Der Apostel* [The Apostle (1890)], *Der Narr in Christo Emanuel Quint* [The Fool in Christ Emanuel Quint (1910)], and *Der Ketzer von Soana* [The Heretic of Soana (1918)]. Each of these works depicts, from a different perspective, the groping attempt of an individual to achieve and maintain an authentic *unio mystica* in a modern world antithetical to such desires and in a natural setting which renders a strictly Christian solution vaguely inadequate. Particularly significant for the depiction of the heroes of all three works is the conflict between the rising claims of psychology in a materialistic society and the belief in a spiritual reality which the author was not prepared to relinquish.

This theme, which can be restated as the problem of clinical versus divine madness, is treated most directly in *Der Apostel.* Almost devoid of plot, the little sketch reflects Hauptmann's personal experience with religious frenzy during his Lederose period, his exposure to the ideas of the psychiatrist Forel in Zürich, the unmistakable influence of Büchner's landmark psychological novella *Lenz* (1835), and a fleeting contact with Johannes Guttzeit, a religious eccentric and vagrant who later accused the author of an unauthorized depiction of himself and his circumstances.[1] Although little more than "a vain and shallow neurotic whose Imitation of Christ is an incidental by-product of narcissism and exhibitionism, ultimately compounded with the unmistakable signs of an Oedipus complex,"[2] the "apostle" of the story is just barely exonerated of outright charlatanism by extenuating circumstances: a fine sensitivity to the magnificent Swiss landscape, a disgust with the vagaries of modern, industrialized civilization, and an apparently genuine attraction to "the holy word-jewel:—World Peace!" (6:82).

Quint

Two decades after the appearance of *Der Apostel* Hauptmann again returned to prose and to the same central theme. *Emanuel Quint* is both his first and most widely acclaimed novel and one of the finest treatments of the "Jesus redivivus" motif in world literature. The unlikely hero's brief religious career leads "through an extraordinarily rich and convincing picture of men, their doings, and their world, a picture as vivid and intense as those Hauptmann achieved in his best plays."[3]

As related by a chronicler who makes no claims to omniscience, the plot unfolds through an unobtrusive frame and depicts—now vaguely, now in great and realistic detail—the last year and a half of the twenty-eight-year-old hero's life. An outcast of society by virtue of his illegitimacy and a suspicion of feeblemindedness, Emanuel Quint suffers additionally at the hands of his stepfather, a cruel, drunken carpenter. In apparent compensation for his dismal existence he begins to draw attention to himself by preaching repentance in the marketplace of a nearby village. In spite of general ridicule he gains a few disciples, generally even less stable than himself, and, although largely inadvertently, finds himself venerated as a faith healer and miracle worker. It is to his credit that he resists the temptation to self-aggrandizement. The essence of his teaching is that God is spirit and therefore accessible to everyone without intermediary. This mystical message proves too subtle for his followers whose deprived personalities crave wonders of a more substantial sort. Once initiated, and in spite of Quint's brief incarceration in an insane asylum, his little movement gathers new adherents, including a noble "Gurauer Fräulein" who sponsors him and provides him with access to more elevated strata of society. Meanwhile, however, his basic and more numerous cadre of "Valley Brethern" gets increasingly out of control. Only his severe sermon at a nocturnal orgy succeeds in discouraging the zealots, leaving him with only a few followers. On his wanderings he next seeks out his natural father, a minister whose church he devastates with the hubristic cry: "I am Christ!" Continuing on to Breslau, he establishes his own "church" in a disreputable tavern where he provides solace for despairing individuals from all walks of life. As his self-confidence in his mission grows, however, most of these followers, disappointed in their hopes for a spiritual rebirth, also fall by the wayside. When the teen-ager Ruth Heidebrand, a gardener's daughter whose fervor for Quint is compounded with a strong erotic infatuation, is sexually molested and murdered, Quint is suspected of the crime and taken into custody. In spite of his confession of guilt, his innocence is (justly) established. This ultimate sacrifice rejected, the delusion of being Christ sustains him a while longer, but a spring thaw, in the vicinity of the St. Gotthard's Pass, brings to light a frozen corpse—presumably his. A scrap of paper found on the body contains only the enigmatic question: "The secret of the Realm?"

On a personal level the work is a *roman à clef* containing numerous barely disguised portraits such as those of the literary agitators Heinrich and Julius Hart (the brothers Hassenpflug), the Bohemian writers Peter Hille and Elsa Lasker-Schüler (Peter Hullenkamp and Annette von Rhyn), the troubled suicide and friend of his youth Dominik (same name), or his own guilt-ridden alter ego from his sojourns in Lohnig and Breslau, Kurt Simon. As a depiction of the zeitgeist, *Quint* records, better than any other literary work, the peculiar blend of Marxist agitation, psychology, Nietzschean exaltation, and the Messianic fervor so characteristic of the turn of the century in Germany.

The basic subject matter was hardly new. Dostoevski, whom Hauptmann had studied intently in Zürich, treats it in *The Idiot* and in the "Grand Inquisitor" episode of *The Brothers Karamazov;* Fritz von Uhde's paintings of Christ among the modern workers of Germany had popularized it; case histories of people who believed themselves to be Christ had been investigated, and Jesus himself was being described as a paranoid. Still, it is hard to imagine an author better equipped to give it artistic expression. Not only had Hauptmann experienced the contemporary socialist-utopian awakening firsthand and among his friends, but, during his own religious crisis, he had known Quint-like itinerants, and had absorbed the language of the New Testament to a point where he could use it unselfconsciously as his own.[4]

Eschewing Naturalism for a heightened, at times magical, realism, Hauptmann skillfully superimposes a biblical ambience upon his poor hero's Silesian landscape. Thus instead of using the dialect one might expect, Quint speaks almost exclusively in biblical quotations, and the author uses a number of Christian character names such as Emanuel

("God is with us"), Johannes, Josef, Nathaniel, Ruth—or the Saints' names Agnes, Hedwig, and Therese—to further enhance the pervasive religious atmosphere. A similar mythologizing strategy is evident in the novel's structure. The events of Quint's life frequently parallel Christ's; a mystical number (seven) of chapters is devoted to each of the main stations of his earthly journey, and the seasons of his "Passion" correspond to those of nature: i.e., "vernal longing, summer fulfillment, autumnal waning, and hibernal congelation."[5] Indeed even the personality of the narrator serves as a moderating, genuinely Christian force. Wise, somewhat skeptical, and ironic, his compassionate understanding raises him and his story above the level of the merely "professional" Christians (cf., especially Pastor Kellwinkel) who make Quint's lot such a difficult one.

Such formal considerations counterpoint the more modern tendencies of the plot, suggest its inherent ambiguity, and serve as a caution against one-sided interpretations. *Quint* is simultaneously an autobiographical novel (in the less superficial sense of that word), a novel of social criticism, a psychological novel, and a novel about the indomitable longing of the human spirit for a transcendental justification of its existence. As autobiography it represents a distillation of Hauptmann's personal experience as it relates to these themes. As a work of social criticism (as which it was almost exclusively seen upon its appearance) it covers much the same ground familiar from the author's Naturalist plays; i.e., the collusion of state, church, and capital to the detriment of the poor. As a psychological study, it explores in impressive detail both the individual and mass psyche; i.e., on the one hand, it provides a detailed analysis of Quint's mental aberrations (on the basis of such now-familiar concepts as oedipal relationship, inferiority complex, and compensation for psychic deprivation) and, on the other, explores the roles of charismatic leadership, madness, and Eros in the perennially recurring phenomenon of mass religious hysteria.

While these modern, almost scientific, aspects of Quint's story play a major role in the novel, they are counterbalanced by a strong mystical element. To be sure, Quint imitates Christ and in his ethical integrity comes close to being a model Christian, but his religion also contains elements which predate the teachings of Jesus. His intense susceptibility to nature, an adoration of the sun which borders on worship, and his almost Dionysian concept of the shepherd, are closer to the Nietzschean view of early Greece than to the Christian tradition. This ambivalence is further enhanced by the fact that his potentially most salient Christian experiences are clouded in uncertainty. Thus, while locked in a cell, he *seems* to achieve *unio mystica,* but, as in the case of the *Apostel,* the event is somewhat suspect since it occurs in a dream. Likewise, the reader is prevented from witnessing Quint's last days and death—a period which would be especially useful in assessing the authenticity of his religiosity. Even the narrator is not completely certain that the body found in the frozen desolation is that of Quint, and the words: "The secret of the Realm?" are more likely to encourage speculation than to end it.

Der Ketzer

Quint was Hauptmann's last predominantly Christian work and, according to a conversation he had with Thomas Mann, he saw it as a fragment in need of a "Dionysian continuation,"[6] which *Der Ketzer von Soana* offers. Begun in 1911, almost immediately after the publication of *Quint,* set in the vicinity of Quint's presumed demise, and featuring a hero who in many ways resembles a more sophisticated "fool in Christ," this short novel soon became the author's most popular prose work.[7] That it is also "undoubtedly his finest prose work and, for that matter, one of the masterpieces of German narrative writing,"[8] as Hugh F. Garten maintains, may be disputed in an age wary of florid pathos and intoxicated emotions; but its impact on the young was similar to that of two other passionate works of modern German literature: Rilke's *Coronet* and Hermann Hesse's *Demian.* Perhaps in order to keep the reader (or himself?) at a safe remove from the more sordid aspects of the plot, the author uses a double frame device. In the Tessin mountains of Switzerland the "editor" of the story hears the shepherd Ludovico, known locally as the heretic of Soana, relate an older tale about Francesco Vela—actually a thinly disguised narration of Ludovico's own experiences. As a young priest so ascetic and devout that he has acquired a reputation as a saint among the folk, Francesco is assigned by his superiors to return to the fold the disreputable Scarabota family, which, because of its patently incestuous habits, is shunned by the villagers and lives high in the mountains in pagan isolation. On his trip into the mountains the magnificent Swiss landscape awakens totally new sensations in the young man: "For the first time [he] felt a clear, grandiose feeling of existence rush through him, which caused him to forget, for moments at a time, that he was a priest and why he had come" (6:108). In Agata, the daughter of the incestuous brother and sister Scarabota, he discovers a beautiful, vital embodiment of this feeling. Even when he returns to the valley below he cannot forget her and is driven to fashion a religion that will expand Christianity through the overwhelming power of passion and nature. The Mass he subsequently holds for the outcasts in an isolated mountain chapel assumes for him the dimensions of such a Christian-pagan synthesis which, however, proves to be quite transitory. A night of love with Agata easily shifts the precarious balance from Christ to Dionysus: "He was no longer master of his life. A powerful magic had made him . . . a completely subservient victim of Eros, of the god who is older and more powerful than Zeus and the other gods" (6:166).

Although parallels to others' works have been detected in it,[9] *Der Ketzer* is an intensely personal confession. Even if one is unwilling to accept it as evidence of Hauptmann's predilection for incest,[10] its intensity is unthinkable without his trip to Greece in 1907 and his intimate familiarity with Italy and the Alps. The name Scarabota pays homage to an Italian beauty with whom he had enjoyed a flirtation some twenty-five years earlier,[11] and Agata's tendency to merge in the hero's imagination with an archetypal "Earth Mother" coincides with Hauptmann's own, idealized conception of the "eternally feminine." As in the case of *Quint,* however, *Der Ketzer* provides no final answers. Ludovico/Francesco, too, is an extreme case, an exploration of a possible path to a richer, deeper life. His main weakness is that, being human, he cannot clearly distinguish between earthbound sex and the more exalted forms of love. "Eros' Song of Songs has, in the final analysis, become a Song of Songs of sex—here secretly disguised as Eros."[12]

Chapter Nine

Exotica

It is characteristic of Hauptmann's middle period—roughly 1906 to 1922—that he preoccupied himself with several works at the same time. Thus *Der Ketzer, Magnus Garbe, Die Winterballade,* and *Der weiße Heiland* [The White Savior (1920)], notwithstanding their depiction of radically different periods, climes, and dramatic situations, were all composed more or less simultaneously.[1]

Der weiße Heiland

The "dramatic fantasy" *Der weiße Heiland* is a verse drama in eleven scenes which illuminates the fateful confrontation between Cortez and Montezuma in sixteenth-century Mexico. Essentially, the plot does little more than provide an imaginative portrait of the last Aztec emperor who, seduced by religious longing, allows his people to be victimized by marauding Spaniards whose motives are also ostensibly religious, but who are in reality crassly mercenary. Their greed for Aztec gold has brought them to a fever pitch of destructive ferocity. Montezuma, revered by his subjects as a son of the sun, is especially vulnerable. World-weary and ready for death, he seizes upon the prediction of his priests that the sun god himself will soon return to earth. Disregarding all warnings to the contrary, he mistakes Cortez and his men (dressed as they are in shining armor and bearing marvelous, fire-spouting weapons) as the longed-for god and his emissaries. By the time he recognizes his mistake it is too late. Under the leadership of the knight Pedro de Alvarado the Spanish forces imprison and slaughter the Aztecs without decisively conquering them. Suddenly the gentle race rises up ferociously against the aggressors and the Spaniards find themselves surrounded. The fact that they hold Montezuma hostage is of little advantage since the Aztecs feel betrayed and in no mood to exchange him for a guarantee of peace with the beleaguered invaders. In the end, dying of wounds inflicted by his own subjects, Montezuma rejects both Cortez's attempt to convert him to Christianity and his offer of reconciliation. In a last heroic effort he tears the bandages from his wounds and damns the Spaniards to destruction.

This sparse plot is luxuriantly fleshed out with lengthy monologues and epic descriptions, and it would be as wrongheaded to demand dramatic consistency of the work as to insist on historical verisimilitude in its execution. Curiously, its spiritual progenitor is Oswald Spengler (*Decline of the West*) and its dominant tone resignation. The supposed cultural achievements of the Spaniards and their orthodox Christianity are by no means superior to the more natural lifestyle and sun-worship of the Aztecs. The invaders too are human under their shining armor, and human sacrifice will continue to be practiced (albeit under varying guises) by both nations. As for Montezuma himself, he is yet another in the long line of Hauptmann heroes seeking eschatological enlightenment; more exotic than Quint but like him half believing in his own divinity, and like Michael Kramer achieving through suffering at least the illusion of a life-affirming epiphany, a glimpse of a distant paradise.

Indipohdi

The "dramatic poem" *Indipohdi* (1920) (Hauptmann also called it a "tragedy")[2] is an exotic companion piece to *Der weiße Heiland*. Again the drama revolves around a "white savior," a positive figure in this instance, and one who shares with Montezuma a similar quasi-divinity, a wisdom of resignation, and a longing for self-sacrifice. As in the preceding play, the contrast between unbridled lust for power and humane wisdom plays a central role, and Prospero, the main character with the Shakespearean name,[3] turns increasingly into an idealized self-portrait of his creator. In contrast to some of his critics who are disturbed by what they consider a lack of adequate dramatic motivation and an excess of literary and cultural ballast, Hauptmann saw his drama, when it was written, as the very personal capstone of his work and as his legacy to the future.[4] Seen from the perspective of what was still to come, this judgment was a bit premature. Henceforth, however, Hauptmann the writer tends to withdraw even more from the external world to the larger problems of theology and the meaning of life;

problems he now tends to explore through the medium of myth and arcane religious lore, in more "difficult," less popular, constructs than his early Naturalist plays.

Originally intended as a kind of paraphrase of Shakespeare's *Tempest*, *Indipohdi* is also variously reminiscent of Jakob Böhme, Plato ("philosopher king"), Buddha, Christ, Friedrich Hölderlin (*Death of Empedocles*), and Goethe (the humanizing influence of Iphigenie among the barbarians). Hauptmann himself saw it as "the deepest and most painful tragedy of all that is human: this road to loneliness and nothingness," and summed up what he considered its dominant emotional tone with the words: "God created the world and then forgot his creation."[5] Again, as in *Der weiße Heiland,* the plot is secondary to the long, lyrical monologues, especially those of Prospero. Like so many of the author's works it centers on family conflict, in this case an intense and unexplained hatred of a son for his father.

Years ago, according to Hauptmann's plot, the noble prince Prospero was driven from his land by his power-hungry son, Ormann. Having found refuge on an isolated island, he has gradually become the spiritual leader of its Indian inhabitants who venerate him as the son of their sun god, the "white savior" of their religion, whose return to earth has long been predicted. By now, however, Prospero has had his fill of life and is prepared to forsake it when he is presented with a final, painful ordeal. His son Ormann (= "gold man") has landed on the same island at the head of a shipwrecked band of gold-seekers. The Indian rebel Amaru declares him the true "white god," and a renewed power struggle between father and son looms. Prospero, meanwhile, ruminates on the inexplicable metaphysical roots of life's suffering and feels helpless in avoiding a final apotheosis of this suffering. Either he must submit in battle to his son, whom, in spite of everything, he still loves, or, in his function as priest-king, he must sacrifice him according to the Indian custom of his adopted land. The fact that Ormann is eventually captured and bound only intensifies Prospero's world-weariness and his urge for self-sacrifice. Like Christ he feels at once innocent yet burdened with the sins of the world, and as he climbs with his beloved priestess Tehura to the peak of the island volcano into which he intends to cast his life he has a revelation. Comparing himself with the legendary Indian king Indipohdi who appeared from the unknown and vanished just as mysteriously into it, and whose name means "no one knows it," he is spiritually prepared to let himself fall into that larger realm which both encompasses and transcends earthly suffering. At this moment Tehura pronounces him divine, and the fact that Ormann, released by command of Prospero before undertaking the climb, follows him to the volcano, cannot break his resolve. He has come to the realization that all his creativity, all his "magic," and all his suffering was preordained by incomprehensible forces beyond his control.

Prospero's words before the scene on the mountain dissolves in fog and the final curtain falls ("I feel you, I sink into you! Nothingness!" [2:1437]) are not to be construed as an absolute nihilism. Indeed, they are more than counterbalanced by the ecstatic tone in which they are spoken and the hero's references to "reconciliation," "music of the spheres," and "star of love" which immediately precede them. The world he is leaving, we are given to believe, is for Prospero less real than the realm of "nothingness" for which the sufferings of life have at last ripened him.

Indipohdi represents an organic stage in Hauptmann's work which is both rooted in the past and projected toward the future. On the one hand, Prospero is a further incarnation of Wann (*Pippa*), who, like bell-founder Heinrich and Quint, struggles to the heights, apostrophizes death (like Michael Kramer), and finally escapes his furies by dissolving into the elements. On the other hand, in its increasingly abstract mythologizing, concern with human sacrifice and divinity, and the gnostic idea of the world as battleground of light and dark forces—of Christ and Dionysus, two brothers who hold each other precariously at bay by virtue of the fact that they have the same father—points directly to the characteristic works of Hauptmann's old age. [6]

Chapter Ten
Sunset and Night

Vor Sonnenuntergang

For Hauptmann 1932 was in some respects the most significant year of his long life. The year-long celebration of his seventieth birthday, which by a kind quirk of fate coincided with the centennial of the death of a "patron saint" of his old age, Johann Wolfgang von Goethe,[1] brought him a harvest of acclaim and honor: the prestigious Goethe Prize of Frankfurt; a theater named after him in Breslau; a celebration and speech by Thomas Mann in his honor in Munich; similar celebrations in Prague, Vienna, Dresden, Hamburg, and Leipzig, to give a representative sampling. By now the most famous author and one of the best-loved personalities in Germany, his renown had reached such proportions that it spilled across the Atlantic and provided the occasion for a second trip to the United States. Here (in addition to providing amusing anecdotal material which has charmed several generations of Germanists since then) he was awarded an honorary doctorate by Columbia University; delivered his lecture on Goethe on that occasion and later at Harvard, in Washington, D.C., and in Baltimore; was presented to Herbert Hoover in the White House, met such luminaries as Theodore Dreiser, Sinclair Lewis, Eugene O'Neill, Helen Keller, and Lillian Gish, and, by all accounts enjoyed himself immensely.[2]

The same year, 1932, brought the premiere of his last great theatrical success, an additional tribute to Goethe with the prophetic title *Vor Sonnenuntergang* [Before Sunset]. Like its "sunrise" companion-piece of forty-three years earlier (*Vor Sonnenaufgang*) it also presaged a new era for Hauptmann and the German people: in this case the rise of fascism under Adolf Hitler who came to power in January, 1933. By July of that year Hauptmann rather accurately concluded: "My epoch begins in 1870 and ends with the burning of the Reichstag."[3] By 1937 a film version of *Vor Sonnenuntergang*, retitled *Der Herrscher* [The Ruler] was being used in the service of Nazi propaganda.

As the play opens, Matthias Clausen, the hero, seems (like his creator) to stand at the pinnacle of worldly success. A wealthy industrialist, owner of a publishing house, and even a respected humanist scholar, his elaborate seventieth birthday celebration seems to confirm his considerable position in the world. To be sure, he has suffered deeply during the last three years after the death of his wife, but a chance encounter with Inken Peters, the niece of a gardener on one of his estates, has given him a new lease on life. In spite of an age difference of half a century and their awareness of the social risks of such a relationship, they have fallen in love. The opposition when it comes, however, does not come from outside the family, but from within. Led by Erich Klamroth, Clausen's son-in-law who already plays a role in directing the Clausen enterprises and wishes to acquire sole control over them, the old man's children, abetted by their rather unsavory spouses, set out to separate the lovers, using blackmail, bribery, slander, and any other weapons at their disposal. In spite of their protestations about the social inappropriateness of the match, their real motive is financial. As daughter Bettina expresses it to her father in a remark heavy with irony: "You are our very greatest treasure . . . we don't want to lose this treasure" (3:335). With the partial exception of the youngest son, Egmont, the children are concerned about losing their inheritance to a new wife. When Clausen and Inken refuse to capitulate and make plans to settle in Switzerland, the family takes measures to have the old man declared legally incompetent on the basis of alleged senility. The shock of seeing the meanness of his children is too much for Clausen, and he kills himself with cyanide in the house of the gardener where he first saw Inken.

Although critics have tried—more or less successfully—to reveal literary connections between *Vor Sonnenuntergang* and works such as Shakespeare's *King Lear,* Goethe's *Marienbad Elegy,* and the author's own *Einsame Menschen, Dorothea Angermann, Die Hochzeit auf Buchenhorst,* and *Im Wirbel der Berufung,*[4] the main inspiration for the drama came from Hauptmann's personal experiences and those of his friends. Since these have been summarized elsewhere,[5] it suffices here to mention a few of the more important ones. On a strictly personal level is the parallel to the May–December marriage of the author's grandfather and to his own association with a young peasant girl named Inken Diedrichsen whom he met in 1915 on the island of Sylt (cf. 7:527). More significant were two long-time friends: Hermann G. Fiedler and Max Pinkus. The former, a professor of German at Oxford who had been instrumental in the award of Hauptmann's first honorary doctorate in 1905, appears in the play as Clausen's supporter and understanding friend Professor Geiger of Cambridge (Fiedler/Geiger = fiddler/ violinist). The latter, Pinkus, served as a model for Clausen himself. An idealistic manufacturer, art patron, and book collector like Clausen, he too had been widowed and had gotten into a bitter conflict with his children over the inheritance of his fortune when, in old age, he fell in love with a young woman.[6]

While a summary of the plot tends to emphasize the "Lear" theme of the ungrateful children, this is not the only theme and perhaps not even the most important one. The play is a rich psychological study of a family in decline; of one daughter (Bettina) who had been physically short-changed and has compensated with an unhealthy relationship to her father; of another delicate, over-refined daughter (Ottilie) who has masochistically married a brute who abuses and deceives her; and of an ineffectual son (Wolfgang) whose abilities are vastly overshadowed by those of his father and who has developed accordingly. While it is dangerous to try to catalogue "themes" in any real work of art, Gerhard Schulz is perhaps close to the mark when he asserts that *Vor Sonnenuntergang* consists of three dramas in one: a love drama, a social drama, and one which can best be described in terms of Hauptmann's concept of the *Urdrama*.[7] The love drama, rather typically for Hauptmann, involves the fateful attraction for a beautiful blonde young woman who, at least in this case, is fully worthy of his love. More complex and interesting is the socially critical level of the play, and it is here that the author's homage to Goethe plays a central role. With increasing age he identified more and more strongly with the great man from Weimar—to the point of stylizing his appearance to resemble Goethe's and referring to himself half-jokingly as his "son."[8] The play is filled with reminders of Goethe (e.g., names associated with him; Goethean quotations; and the common knowledge that the seventy-three-year-old Goethe also fell in love with a girl more than fifty years his junior). Clausen is a virtual embodiment of Goethe's "pure humanity" which comes into conflict with the brutally materialistic way of life personified by Eric Klamroth, a way of life which rejects cultural sensitivity and values as useless baggage and stresses "progress," the accumulation of money and power by any means, and the "survival of the fittest." The apparent victory of such a mentality seems in retrospect a prophetic foreshadowing of the dark era of German history which was just beginning.

The *Urdrama* "that life secretly always holds . . . in readiness, even for Fortune's favorite," in this case Clausen, is, like so much of the play, also reminiscent of earlier work—*Michael Kramer,* for example. Although Clausen had considered suicide after the death of his wife (there was something in the idea of "relaxation, rest, indeed of an undeniable ecstasy" [3:297]), he had been able to resist it. Only after coming to know the true abyss of suffering at the hands of his children, a suffering which brings him to the edge of madness, does he achieve that final illumination that reduces the distinction between life and death to a matter of indifference.

Das Meerwunder

Of Hauptmann's later prose works the sixty-odd page narrative *Das Meerwunder. Eine unwahrscheinliche Geschichte* [The Sea Miracle: An Improbable Story (1934)] exemplifies especially well the pessimism of his old age. Written during the depressing early years of the Hitler regime, it is another frame story allegedly based on events encountered many years earlier in a seaport of Italy by the author himself. Having made the acquaintance of an erstwhile candidate for the priesthood, an eccentric collector of dubious curios named Otonieri, the young author is introduced to a strange society of *Lichtstümpfe* (the name means "candle stumps" and refers to the all-but-burned-out lives of its members).

By far the most remarkable member of this group is a dying sea captain, variously called Mausehund and Cardenio; and it is his report to the society that the author records for posterity. As in the plays *Cardenio and Celinde* of Andreas Gryphius and Karl Immermann, Cardenio steals another man's woman, falls completely under her demonic spell, and finds himself embraced by a skeleton. After the mysterious death of the young beauty—whom he calls Seekatze or Chimaera—Cardenio carves a ships' figurehead in her image and sails with it as far as the South Pacific where he is shipwrecked on a deserted island together with his idol and the ship's cook, Sarrazin. Wracked by tropical fever, he becomes obsessed with a belief in the resurrection of his enchanted maiden. For him she is one of those mythological *femmes fatales,* like Undine or Melusine, who long to be human—to their own regret.

All too soon Chimaera recognizes her mistake. The sacrifice of innocence and grace for the dubious advantages of humanity bring her to a depth of despair in which she cries out: "I don't want to be human!" (6:398). Not only does she reject humanity, but she influences Cardenio to reject it also. His eyes opened, he bitterly observes: "I only saw the ugly, the disgusting, and that I had ever considered anything beautiful in this uniformly horrible world, I could, transformed as I was, no longer understand. . . . In short, I no longer saw the bright, cheerfully optimistic pennant of the ship of mankind, but a black one, dyed in blood" (6:399).

Gladly he would renounce the supposed advantages of civilization if he could only submerge himself in the elementary, animalistic world of Chimaera, a foretaste of whose incomprehensible bliss he is magically granted by being transformed into a playful triton with a beautiful Nereid astride his powerful back. The narrative ends amid the grotesque reality of the *Lichtstümpfe.* Having for the first time confessed his story to the members of the society, Cardenio destroys the wooden Chimaera and ritualistically consigns it to the flames. As the last splinter is devoured by them, he too seems to collapse into ashes.

First impressions to the contrary, *Das Meerwunder* does not represent a radical departure for Hauptmann, and its differences from earlier works are differences more of degree than of kind. Thus, to begin with an obvious parallel, the much earlier drama *Gabriel Schillings Flucht* [Gabriel Schilling's Flight], written in 1905–6, anticipates much of the atmosphere and a number of motifs of the story. Here too, in the manner of Arnold Böcklin, the sea is mythologized and given a central role as the ultimate source and destination of mankind. In both works a ship's figurehead assumes a life of its own and is closely identified with a dark-haired vampiric woman who leads the hero to nervous collapse and destruction.

Further parallels can be traced back to such seemingly disparate prose works as *Der Ketzer, Thiel,* and even *Fasching,* particularly as in the first two works the hero also retreats with a sensual woman to a magnificent but isolated physical setting conducive to introspection and hallucination. In each case the natural surroundings dwarf human existence and prepare the ground for a paranormal experience; and in each case an animalistic woman (or one very much at home with animals) is responsible for a radical but ambiguous change in the life and outlook of the hero (ambiguous because of the abnormal circumstances such as dreams, visions, insanity, etc. under which it is accomplished). Although unwilling to define clearly the line of demarcation between them, Hauptmann, in each of these works and in many others, posits the existence of two distinct realms: the gray, dull realm of day-to-day existence and another dark, dangerous primeval world under the surface to which exceptional individuals find their way, at the cost of orthodox faith and, perhaps, of sanity and life.

For Hauptmann, as for Freud, civilization is responsible for inhibiting a free expression of Western man's sensuality and therefore of placing unnecessary constraints upon his creativity and upon an important part of his life. According to Sarrazin, humanity has taken a fateful wrong turn. Instead of evolving into a *Menschentier* ("man-animal") with the highly developed attributes and abilities of other animals, man is burdened with an excess of rationality. Mausehund, with his revealing animalistic name ("Mousedog,") recapitulates this ideal evolution whose goal is the "dismantling of a certain super-morality and tormenting super-intellectuality which create useless pains and sufferings" (6:382). As in the case of bell-founder Heinrich—whose love for a quasi-human sprite also opened new vistas—Cardenio/Mausehund, however, is too weak, or too much the victim of civilization, to survive his elevation to the semi-divine realm of Chimæra. As a human being, he is consumed by the intensity of her existence and the experiment undertaken with him ends in failure. The projected *Menschentier* expires as a burned-out *Lichtstumpf* in madness and ashes.

Atriden-Tetralogie

Hauptmann's last dramatic work, the *Atriden-Tetralogie,* has been praised as "the highpoint of [his] artistic development"[9] and, in spite of apparent weaknesses as a stage play, "as the most magnificent accomplishment of the German spirit [Geist]"[10] of its era. Essentially a ten-act drama in four parts, it represents the author's very personal treatment of the Agamemnon legend. Written during World War II, it consists, in intended order (but not in order of completion), of four closely related tragedies: *Iphigenie in Aulis* (1942), *Agamemnons Tod* [Agamemnon's Death (1942)], *Elektra* (1944), and *Iphigenie in Delphi* (1940). Abbreviated plot summaries of the four plays follow:

Iphigenie in Aulis. The Greek army, led by Agamemnon, is trying to embark for Troy to avenge the abduction of Helena but is unable to do so. The goddess Artemis has becalmed the sea and subjected Aulis to terrible heat and drought because Agamemnon killed her beloved sacred hind during a hunt. The seer Kalchas has a solution: the goddess can be appeased if the king will sacrifice his daughter on Artemis's altar. Under the pretext that the daughter, Iphigenie, is to be married to Achilleus, Agamemnon has her and her mother, Klytämnestra, brought to his camp. However, Peitho, Iphigenie's nursemaid and companion, sees through the ruse. The arrival of a black ship with blood-red sails from her barbarian homeland signals the presence of Hekate (the Tauric Artemis) and means that Iphigenie is in imminent danger. Klytämnestra struggles with her husband over the life of her daughter, but when she sees that, blinded by ambition to lead his expeditionary force to Troy, he is willing to sacrifice even their child, she turns from him. Iphigenie herself is not only willing to be sacrificed, but falls into a state of ecstatic delirium over having been chosen by the goddess for the honor. Before the sacrifice can take place, however, she is led away by three mysterious crones, representatives of Hekate. A hind is placed on the altar in her stead, and Agamemnon, in a trance-like state, kills it without noticing the substitution.

Agamemnons Tod. Ten years have passed, and Klytämnestra is ruling over Mykene with her lover Aigisthos. A rumor that the Greek army has been defeated before Troy, and that Agamemnon is dead, turns out to be false; he has conquered and destroyed the city and is returning home with rich booty. Also in the kingdom of Mykene, and about to take leave of one another in a temple, are Elektra and Orest, the sister and brother of Iphigenie, who has been removed to Tauris. Dismayed by his mother's acceptance of Aigisthos and the latter's usurpation of the reign of the legitimate king, Orest has decided to leave. Sensing that her father is still alive, Elektra stays and finds her intuition confirmed when a powerfully built beggar, accompanied by another man and a badly dressed woman, appears at the temple seeking asylum. The strangers turn out to be Agamemnon, his faithful servant

Kritolaos, and Kassandra, a Trojan princess and seer. They have been shipwrecked and cast ashore without knowing where they are. Eventually Agamemnon reveals his identity, but the touching reunion is interrupted by the approach of Klytämnestra for her nocturnal prayer to the goddess of death, Persephoneia, in whose realm she believes Iphigenie to dwell. After some doubt Klytämnestra recognizes the beggar as the "murderer" of her child. Kassandra predicts that she herself will die at the hands of Aigisthos and that Klytämnestra will slay Agamemnon. With feigned subservience Klytämnestra leads Agamemnon to a holy bath in the inner temple. When Aigisthos arrives and asks about the whereabouts of his queen, Kassandra tells him she is with her husband and is slain on the spot for her pains. From the bath we hear a terrible scream. Klytämnestra has split Agamemnon's head with an axe. With the bloody weapon raised above her head she proclaims the avenging of Iphigenie's death and her willingness to accept, henceforth, superhuman suffering for her deed. The elders of Mykene, who have, in the meantime, arrived to pay their respects to Agamemnon, call, together with Elektra, for Orest to revenge the slaughter.

Elektra. More years pass. The temple is dilapidated, and a stinking vapor rises from the fateful bath. Orest, fearful of an oracle which has predicted that he will kill his mother, has fled Delphi with his friend Pylades and, without recognizing it, seeks shelter in the very temple where his father died. While reminiscing about the possibility that Elektra may still be alive, the two are startled by her appearance, dressed in rags, from behind the ruins of an idol. Since the death of Agamemnon the thought of revenge has kept her at the scene of the murder. From her Orest learns that he is indeed destined to kill his mother. Suddenly a storm arises, bringing Aigisthos and Klytämnestra to the temple for shelter. When confronted with the axe she had used to kill her husband, Klytämnestra admits her guilt and proclaims her readiness to be reconciled with her children—even to the point of returning to Orest his right to the throne in Argos. Enraged, Aigisthos tries to intervene but is slain by Pylades. Klytämnestra collapses but then rallies to curse her children. Ferociously she attacks Orest, struggles with him offstage to the bath, from whence we hear her screams. When Orest returns he hands his sister the axe covered with the blood of their slain mother. As the act closes, it is plain that Elektra has lost her grip on reality.

Iphigenie in Delphi.   All three acts of this fourth part of the tetralogy take place at the temple of Apollo in Delphi. Through a conversation between the priests, Prorors and Aiakoas, we learn that, for the purpose of atonement, an impossibly difficult task has been imposed upon Orest: he must capture and bring to Apollo in Delphi the statue of the goddess Artemis from the barbarous country of Tauris, the land of the gruesome Hekate. Elektra arrives with the axe which killed her father and her mother, in order to return it to Apollo, upon whose command Orest had slain Klytämnestra. She offers herself as a sacrifice if the gods will let Orest live. Shortly thereafter a young man with snow-white hair and a face ravaged by suffering appears and places an oar upon the same altar where Elektra has deposited the axe. It is Orest (calling himself Theron) who claims that Orest and his friend Pylades have been sacrificed to Hekate in Tauris. Pykron, the high priest, cannot believe him since he is privy to the conditions which have been imposed on Orest for his salvation, and soon learns from Pylades that the image of the goddess has already been captured and is safely aboard ship.

Meanwhile "Theron" has informed Elektra that the priestess who killed Orest (and numerous Greeks) on the altar has been abducted and is also aboard a Greek ship. Within the temple preparations are made for the return of the idol. As the procession bearing the statue of Artemis approaches, it is accompanied by the imposing figure of a high priestess. Elektra tries to attack the latter with the fateful axe— believing her responsible for her brother's death. Pylades prevents this additional bloodshed by telling her and Orest that, the act of atonement having been accomplished, they should awaken from their madness. Orest recovers his sanity and, for the first time, mentions his own name and that of his sister—whereupon Elektra falls into a swoon. The high priestess is none other than Iphigenie, who, since the day she was supposedly sacrificed by Agamemnon, has carried out the bloody rituals of her dark goddess Hekate and can no longer return to Apollo's realm of light. Elektra, recovered from her madness, asks her forgiveness for having raised the axe against her. Iphigenie forgives her and Orest (who, back in Tauris, had threatened her with his sword) as well. She recognizes the two as her brother and sister after Elektra, in a trance, speaks of their long-forgotten childhood. Momentarily

Iphigenie's strange nature, acquired during the years of obedience to her dark goddess, recedes and she kisses Elektra with the words: "My sweet little sister" (3:1083). Then, however, she reveals that her abode is with Persephoneia in the land of the dead and that she will return there. While Orest is given back the kingship of his father's city and, with Pylades and Elektra, can look forward to a new life, Iphigenie throws herself into a ravine, finally attaining the sacrificial death long ago ordained for her.

Written, as it was, amidst the brutality and terror of Hitler's Third Reich, at a time when Hauptmann was more than eighty years old, the tetralogy represents a very personal interpretation of traditional materials. And while it would be an overstatement to claim that he used a Classical legend to express his distaste for the Hitler regime,[11] the dark mood of his work owes as much to that nightmare as to an ingrained fatalism exacerbated now by his own approaching death.

Doubtless due to its striking depiction of basic human problems (e.g., guilt and salvation, love and revenge, crime and punishment), the tragedy precipitated by Agamemnon has provoked a tradition of literary treatment by successive generations of writers willing to risk comparison with an elite of their calling. From the Greek dramatists Aeschylus, Euripides, and Sophocles, to such moderns as Racine, Goethe, Hofmannsthal, O'Neill, Giraudoux, and Sartre, each generation has left its characteristic imprint on the materials.[12]

Because Hauptmann credits some remarks by Goethe with having provided the impetus for his work, and because his adulation for him led to such imitative efforts as *Das Märchen* [The Fairy Tale (1941)] and *Mignon* (1947), one might also be tempted to see the tetralogy as little more than an epigonic tribute. Nothing would be further from the mark. Notwithstanding its author's admiration for Goethe's reliance on "pure humanity" to "redeem all human failings," Hauptmann's universe is too bleak and chaotic to be adequately depicted in terms of the "noble simplicity" and "quiet grandeur" of German Classicism. Written in the age of Freud and Jung, it is closer to the bitter skepticism of Shakespeare's *Hamlet* (especially in the figure of Orest);[13] to the metaphysical confusion and brutality of Kleist's *Penthesilea;* to the Dionysian frenzy of Nietzsche, and to his own view of drama expressed in *Griechischer Frühling*. Indeed, his quest for the roots of tragedy takes him back beyond Euripides, beyond Aeschylus even, to the elements of an archetypal theater of ritual and ceremonial.[14]

Seen from this perspective, the *Atriden-Tetralogie* represents Hauptmann's most intense and successful attempt to express in practice his idea of the *Urdrama,* the ceaseless struggle for supremacy of primeval forces—light vs. darkness, Apollo vs. Hekate, the "gold-ivory Zeus" vs. the "black Zeus," affirmation vs. negation, life vs. death. In this struggle mere human beings are the pawns of powers ultimately beyond their control. Like Agamemnon, who slays the hind of Artemis in the exuberance of the hunt, and thereby initiates the inexorable chain of slaughter, they are at best only darkly aware of their metaphysical guilt; and like the sensitive, artistic youth Orest who kills his mother, they are powerless to resist the preordained orbit of their fate. While the concepts of modern psychology (identity problem, Oedipus complex, psychosis) may be useful in elucidating the interpersonal relationships of the various characters, it is the age-old religious problem, the meaning of man's existence and his relationship to transcendental forces, which receives the heaviest emphasis.

That Hauptmann fails to provide a definitive answer to this problem should no longer come as a surprise. His serious dramas are all variations on the struggle between light and darkness, and in the tetralogy the shift is decidedly toward the latter. That human beings are only the tools of the gods, who use them for their own selfish interests, is already suggested by the fact that the decisive highpoints of all four plays are structured around characters who are not in control of their actions: who act in trance-like states, who are touched by madness, or who fall into (or awaken from) unconsciousness. In addition, the dream-like nature of life is frequently evoked and the overall impression is that rationality is incompatible with a true comprehension of the human predicament.

Upon closer inspection, the ending of *Iphigenie in Delphi* does little to correct this imbalance. Although it ends in bright daylight and the characters seem to recover their identity, other factors should not be slighted. On the one hand, one must recall that this drama was the first of the four to be written and reflects a more optimistic outlook than Hauptmann was capable of during the later years of the war. On the other hand, while it signals an end to a particular cycle of fate, Iphigenie's death is ambiguous. Certain overtones of a *Liebestod* ("love death")[15] notwithstanding, it is neither a sacrificial death on behalf of humanity or even primarily on behalf of Orest and Elektra. Depending on the perspective, it is a final act preordained by the gods, or if, contrary to the tendency of the entire work, an element of free will is introduced, it is a selfish act. Iphigenie dies for herself in that, by returning to the realm of Persephoneia as she had dreamed she would (3:1084), she enhances her own already semi-divine nature.[16]

As one would expect in a "dramatic ballad,"[17] atmosphere is at least as important as plot for the artistic success of the tetralogy. This atmosphere, in turn, derives from the structure and form of the dramas—individually and collectively. And while an element of symmetry, suggesting the perfection of fate, is provided by repetition and the dominant image of the circle (e.g., the action begins in Greece and ends there; it begins with an impending counterfeit sacrifice and ends with an accomplished real one), a considerable amount of dissonance is also suggested by Hauptmann's style. Although he used a Classicist iambic pentameter, his intent was not the stately harmony often associated with this meter in German verse. Aiming for a more agitated, emotionally charged language, he often consciously retained lines with too few or too many feet,[18] juxtaposed crassly Naturalistic imagery with beautiful hymnic verse, and archaisms with modern colloquialisms. More concerned with coarsening a material that had become too smooth in its various manifestations through the years, he tends even to be careless about logical motivation[19] in preference for a pathologically askew aura of magic and mythos.

Further enhancing this aura is a complex array of significant sounds, colors, movements, animals, names, objects, and numbers which can only be sampled here. Among the most obvious of these are the use of the "magic" number three throughout the work, the colors black and red with which Hekate is identified, and the murder weapon, the fateful axe, which, as in the German *Schicksalstragödie* ("fate tragedy"), seems subject to a lurid destiny of its own. The darkness that envelops *Agamemnons Tod* and *Elektra* is especially appropriate for these two dramas; the sound of barking dogs, croaking frogs, screeching owls and jackdaws, signifies the breakthrough of otherworldly forces into the earthly realm; and the use of dance, no less than in *Pippa*, alludes to the dithyrambic substratum of life itself.[20] Even the name Iphigenie, finally, is made to yield new dimensions. By intentionally confounding it with the much older form Iphianassa, from a deeper level of the myth in which Hekate, Artemis, and Persephoneia still merge as nature deities, Hauptmann stresses the archetypal roots of his heroine.[21]

If one compares the *Atriden-Tetralogie* with Hauptmann's earlier work, the differences once more turn out to be more apparent than real. Similarities pertain to small details of form (e.g., the use of dance, significant colors and names, animal imagery) as well as to its overall structure (i.e., quite similar architectonics).[22] They also apply, however, to a central premise of his oeuvre: the paradox that, while man must continually struggle against his fate, he is no match for it. The tragedy of Elektra, Orest, and Iphigenie is essentially that of Thiel, Hannele, Henschel, or Rose Bernd. Whether expressed in terms of scientific determinism or in terms of the Greek goddess Nemesis, all of these characters are victims and captives of a fate from which the only escape lies in personal extinction.[23]

Chapter Eleven
A Hauptmann Perspective

As his last works suggest, Hauptmann's final years were hardly cheerful. Having been excluded more and more from the political and literary life of his country, his mood was further darkened by ill health and the ravages of war—he witnessed, firsthand, the destruction of Dresden on February 13, 1945. Although he survived the war his spirit was broken, and he died of pneumonia on June 6, 1946. His body lies interred in the cemetery of the village of Kloster on the island of Hiddensee, the scene of many of his happiest hours.

If, after having surveyed Hauptmann's life and work, we succumb to the critic's very human desire to impose upon it some semblance of order, we must do so with the realization that the task is somewhat akin to reducing to a common denominator the figures of a revolving kaleidoscope. Perhaps the most fruitful approach is to accept the author's assertion that everything he wrote is deeply autobiographical; that for him, as for Goethe, the individual works are but "fragments of a great confession," and therefore, ipso facto, the organic product of a particular man, living under unique circumstances, at a particular time, and in a particular place.

On the very basic level of personal background, relationships, and events, we have seen how Hauptmann's experiences and attitudes have insinuated themselves into his work, often with the regularity of recurrent themes. For example, *Das Friedensfest, Einsame Menschen, Michael Kramer, Der weiße Heiland,* and even the *Atriden-Tetralogie,* are family tragedies with more or less strongly profiled autobiographical overtones which explore the often brutal relationships of family members to each other. Similarly, the at once archetypal and personal man—woman relationship—the destructive and/or redemptive power of Eros—is illuminated in such disparate works as *Thiel, Einsame Menschen, Hannele, Der arme Heinrich, Henschel, Rose Bernd, Pippa, Der Ketzer, Vor Sonnenuntergang,* and *Das Meerwunder,* while others, such as *Das Friedensfest, Die versunkene Glocke, Michael Kramer, Gabriel Schillings*

Flucht, and *Die Ratten* are concerned, to a greater or lesser extent, with the divergent claims of art and life. That other, somewhat less universal, themes also recur is hardly surprising. The social, scientific, political, and religious upheavals of a nation rushing into industrialization find expression in *Vor Sonnenaufgang, Einsame Menschen, Die Weber, Der rote Hahn, Die Ratten, Quint,* and *Vor Sonnenuntergang* (to mention just a few obvious examples).

By analogy the author's travels and his familiarity with different landscapes and countries contribute immeasurably to the atmosphere and artistic integrity of his work. *Rose Bernd* and *Quint* derive a great deal from the Lederose experience; *Pippa* and *Der Ketzer* would be weaker without Hauptmann's trips to Italy; *Der Biberpelz* and *Die Ratten* would hardly be the same without the experience of Berlin; *Schilling, Das Meerwunder,* and the utopian novel *Die Insel der Großen Mutter* [The Island of the Great Mother (1924)] reflect numerous vacations on the island of Hiddensee, and even the *Atriden-Tetralogie* seems to have gained from the direct experience of Greece.

It will not do, of course, to distinguish too precisely between direct personal experiences and those acquired through reading or a kind of osmosis of the zeitgeist. A voracious reader, Hauptmann was influenced (we shall never know exactly to what extent) by such authors as Büchner, Ibsen, Goethe, Shakespeare, Sophocles, and Tolstoy. He was familiar with arcane religious lore from several continents and centuries; immersed himself at different times in the history and literature of the Middle Ages or the nineteenth century; was on intimate terms with the folklore of the *Riesengebirge* area; and had an excellent knowledge of the New Testament. Philosophical influences are equally varied, whether acquired directly or through intermediaries. His work suggests exposure to the thoughts of Plato, Spinoza, Hegel, Nietzsche, Johann Jakob Bachofen, and especially to Schopenhauer and the Silesian mystic Jakob Böhme.

Such (necessarily incomplete) listings can do little more than suggest something of the breadth of Hauptmann's interests. "A poor man such as Hamlet," always conscious of the precariousness and ineffability of the human predicament, he was innately suspicious of final answers. For this reason it is dangerous to make categorical statements about his ultimate beliefs. His individual works must be seen as experiments in search of elusive truths, stressing now one side of a question, now another. It is safer to speak of general tendencies in his outlook than of convictions. Thus, a strong streak of irrationalism (the feeling that reason alone is inadequate for achieving truth) predisposed him to a Romantic apperception—although superficially, much of his best work seems to put him firmly in the Naturalist camp. Similarly, a predisposition to believe in a transcendent realm, an inkling of which is available to human beings only rarely and often at the cost of great suffering, inhibited occasional nihilistic tendencies. Through suffering man is brought to the realization of his insignificance, but he also learns that there are forces beyond his comprehension which, for better or worse, control his fate. The depiction of the workings of fate, indeed, is one of the least disputable constants of Hauptmann's oeuvre. From *Fasching* to the *Atriden-Tetralogie* man's actions are shown as determined by inscrutable forces. That these forces assume different guises (e.g., heredity and environment in *Vor Sonnenaufgang,* religion in *Quint,* Eros in *Der Ketzer,* or naked *Fatum* in the *Atriden-Tetralogie*) does nothing to negate their validity. And while one may deplore the fact that too often this outlook seems to have carried over into his personal life, making him, for example, willing to accept as inevitable the Nazi take-over of Germany, it must be seen as an integral part of his work.

It would be a distortion, of course, to end a study of Hauptmann with an all-too-narrow focus on his ideas. His real contribution lies in his undisputed artistry, especially his genius for the theater. Today, some thirty-five years after his death, he remains—after such classic writers as Goethe, Schiller, and Kleist—one of Germany's most popular playwrights, with every indication that he has found a permanent niche in the history of German literature.

Notes and References

Preface

1. Cf. Karl S. Guthke, "Hauptmann im Hauptmann-Jahr: Sammelreferat . . . ," *Göttingische Gelehrte Anzeigen* 214 (1964): 219.
2. For an international perspective see Lilian R. Furst and Peter N. Skrine, *Naturalism* (London, 1971); for an overview of the German situation see Richard Hamann and Jost Hermand, *Naturalismus* (Munich: Nymphenburg, 1973), Günther Mahal, *Naturalismus* (Munich: Fink, 1975), and Roy Pascal, *From Naturalism to Expressionism: German Literature and Society 1880–1918* (New York: Basic Books, 1973); for German Naturalist drama see Sigfrid Hoefert, *Das Drama des Naturalismus* (Stuttgart: Metzler, 1968); and for a brief introduction to the movement see Warren R. Maurer, *The Naturalist Image of German Literature . . .* (Munich, 1972), pp. 13–44.

Chapter One

1. Rudolf Alexander Schröder, quoted by Bernhard Zeller in *Gerhart Hauptmann: Leben und Werk: Gedächtnisaustellung . . .* , ed. by Bernhard Zeller (Marbach, 1962), p. 8. Henceforth cited as Zeller, *Leben.*
2. Hermann J. Weigand, "Gerhart Hauptmann's Range as Dramatist," *Monatshefte* 44 (1952): 317, cited later as Weigand, "Range."
3. See Eberhard Hilscher, *Gerhart Hauptmann* (Berlin, 1969), p. 5, (hereafter cited as Hilscher, *G. H.*), and Hans Daiber, *Gerhart Hauptmann . . .* (Vienna/Munich/Zürich, 1971), p. 7 (hereafter cited as Daiber, *G. H.*).
4. Ralph Fiedler, *Die späten Dramen Gerhart Hauptmanns . . .* (Munich, 1954), p. 135.
5. Walter Muschg, *Die Zerstörung der deutschen Literatur,* 3d ed. (Berne: Francke, 1958), p. 20.
6. For Hauptmann's influence abroad see Sigfrid Hoefert, *Gerhart Hauptmann* (Stuttgart, 1974), pp. 112–14 (hereafter cited as Hoefert, *G. H.*).
7. See Daiber, *G. H.,* p. 231; Zeller, *Leben,* p. 269, and Frederick W. J. Heuser, *Gerhart Hauptmann . . .* (Tübingen, 1961), p. 91 (hereafter cited as Heuser, *G. H.*).
8. See Paul Böckmann, "Der Naturalismus Gerhart Hauptmanns," in *Interpretationen,* ed. Jost Schillement (Frankfurt, 1966), 2:270; Paul Fechter, *Gerhart Hauptmann* (Dresden, 1922), p. 136; John Osborne, *The*

Naturalist Drama in Germany (Manchester/Totowa, N.J., 1971), p. 35, and Ursula Münchow, *Deutscher Naturalismus* (Berlin: Akademie, 1968), p. 109.

    9. Zeller, *Leben,* p. 10.

    10. Cf. Rolf Michaelis, *Der schwarze Zeus* . . . (Berlin, 1962), p. 38.

    11. Furst and Skrine, *Naturalism,* p. 64.

    12. Quoted by F. A. Voigt, *Gerhart Hauptmann der Schlesier* (Munich: Bergstadt, 1953), p. 67.

    13. Zeller, *Leben,* p. 268, and Daiber, *G. H.,* p. 9.

    14. Citations in parentheses are from the *Centenar* ed. of *Gerhart Hauptmann: Sämtliche Werke,* 11 vols., eds. Hans-Egon Hass and Martin Machatzke (Frankfurt/M., 1966–74).

    15. Carl F. W. Behl and Felix A. Voigt, *Chronik von Gerhart Hauptmanns Leben und Schaffen* (Munich, 1957), p. 26.

    16. Ibid., p. 28.

Chapter Two

    1. Daiber, *G. H.,* p. 38.

    2. Hilscher, *G. H.,* p. 97.

    3. Cf. Hoefert, *G. H.,* p. 13.

    4. For an interpretation of the name Kielblock see Ida H. Washington, "The Symbolism of Contrast in Gerhart Hauptmann's 'Fasching,'" *German Quarterly* 52 (1979): 248. For the autobiographical basis of the remaining names see Warren R. Maurer, "Gerhart Hauptmann's Character Names," *German Quarterly* 52 (1979):461–62.

    5. See, for example, Michael Georg Conrad, *Von Emile Zola bis Gerhart Hauptmann* (Leipzig: Friedrich, 1902), p. 78.

    6. Cf. Behl and Voigt, *Chronik,* p. 24.

    7. Zeller, *Leben,* p. 356.

    8. Cf. also Hilscher, *G. H.,* pp. 99–100, and Walter Silz, *Realism and Reality* . . . (Chapel Hill: University of North Carolina, 1954), pp. 141, 165.

    9. See Silz, *Realism,* pp. 137, 143–44; Roy C. Cowen, *Der Naturalismus* . . . (Munich, 1973), pp. 145–46; and Fritz Martini, *Das Wagnis der Sprache* . . . (Stuttgart, 1954), p. 77.

    10. Maurer, *Naturalist Image,* pp. 226–28.

    11. Silz, *Realism,* p. 146. Cf. Hilscher, *G. H.,* p. 98. For a detailed comparison of Büchner's *Lenz* and *Woyzeck* with *Thiel* see Heinz Fischer, *Georg Büchner: Untersuchungen und Marginalien* (Bonn: Bouvier, 1972), pp. 41–61.

    12. Irene Heerdegen, "Gerhart Hauptmanns Novelle 'Bahnwärter Thiel,'" *Weimarer Beiträge* 3 (1958): 353, 359.

13. Ibid., 359–60.

14. Jean Jofen, *Das letzte Geheimnis* . . . (Berne, 1972), p. 51.

15. Ibid., p. 237, and Dieter Bänsch, "Naturalismus und Frauenbewegung," in *Naturalismus* . . ., ed. Helmut Scheuer (Stuttgart/Berlin/Cologne/Mainz, 1974), pp. 142–43.

16. Silz, *Realism,* p. 148.

17. See Martini, *Wagnis,* pp. 66–69, 91; Benno von Wiese, "Gerhart Hauptmann," in *Deutsche Dichter der Moderne* . . . , ed. Benno von Wiese (Berlin, 1965), p. 29; Karl S. Guthke, *Gerhart Hauptmann* . . . (Göttingen, 1961), p. 54.

18. Erwin T. Rosenthal, "Aspekte der dramatischen Struktur der beiden Tragödien Büchners," *German Quarterly* 38 (1965): 284.

19. Cf. Guthke, *G. H.,* p. 56.

Chapter Three

1. See Hilscher, *G. H.,* pp. 109–10; Hoefert, *G. H.,* p. 14; Osborne, *Naturalist Drama,* pp. 78, 84–85: Hans Mayer, *Hauptmann,* 3d ed. (Velber, 1973), p. 35; and Walter A. Reichart, "Grundbegriffe im dramatischen Schaffen Gerhart Hauptmanns," *PMLA* 82 (1967): 144.

2. Cf. Reichart, ibid., p. 143 and 11:495.

3. Zeller, *Leben,* p. 52.

4. Hilscher, *G. H.,* p. 111, and Behl and Voigt, *Chronik,* p. 32.

5. See Behl and Voigt, *Chronik,* p. 30; Conrad, *Emile Zola,* p. 80, and Maurer, *Naturalist Image,* esp. pp. 39–43.

6. Hilscher, *G. H.,* pp. 103–5, and Zeller, *Leben,* pp. 60–61.

7. Daiber, *G. H.,* p. 52.

8. Quoted by Hilscher, p. 106. See also Theodor Fontane, "Gerhart Hauptmann, 'Vor Sonnenaufgang,'" in *Gerhart Hauptmann,* ed. by Hans Joachim Schrimpf (Darmstadt, 1976), pp. 10–18.

9. See 7:896, 897, 1004; Behl and Voigt, *Chronik,* pp. 15, 22, 26, and Heuser, *G. H.,* pp. 27–29.

10. See 7:880–81, 837–38, 1065; and Osborne, *Naturalist Drama,* pp. 86–87.

11. Fontane, "Gerhart Hauptmann . . .," p. 13.

12. Carl F. W. Behl, *Zwiesprache mit Gerhart Hauptmann* . . . (Munich, 1949), p. 121.

13. Name and character appear to be based on a young woman of Hauptmann's acquaintance. See 7:604.

14. Cf. Osborne, *Naturalist Drama,* p. 86.

15. Cf. Hoefert, *G. H.,* p. 15, for a summary of critical views on him.

16. Osborne, *Naturalist Drama,* p. 89.

17. 1:101. See also Zeller, *Leben,* pp. 62, 64.

18. Neville E. Alexander, *Studien zum Stilwandel* . . . (Stuttgart, 1964), p. 39.

19. See Heuser, *G. H.,* pp. 226–46.

20. Hilscher, *G. H.,* p. 113.

21. Guthke, *G. H.,* p. 68.

22. Cf. also Alexander, pp. 45, 74.

23. Cf. Hilscher, *G. H.,* pp. 126–34, and Heuser, *G. H.,* p. 234. Wolff sees the unresolved outcome of Wilhelm and Ida's relationship as a reflection of the author's own marital problems: i.e., the older generation reflects his fears while the younger personifies his hopes for reconciliation. In Karl S. Guthke and Hans M. Wolff, *Das Leid im Werke Hauptmanns* . . . (Berkeley/ Los Angeles, 1958), p. 63.

24. Heuser, *G. H.,* p. 235.

25. Jofen, *Das letzte,* p. 76.

26. Cf. Heuser, *G. H.,* p. 229.

27. See esp. 7:543–44, and the fragment *Bahnhofstragödie* (*Railway Station Tragedy*), 9:136–37.

28. See Maurer, *Naturalist Image,* p. 44.

29. See Behl, *Zwiesprache,* p. 70; Zeller, *Leben,* pp. 66–67, and Sigfrid Hoefert, "Gerhart Hauptmann und andere" . . . in Scheuer, pp. 246–47.

30. For these and other influences see Daiber, *G. H.,* p. 64; Hilscher, *G. H.,* p. 115; Hoefert, *G. H.,* p. 20; Mayer, *Hauptmann,* p. 39, and Leroy R. Shaw, *The Playwright & Historical Change* (Madison/Milwaukee/London: University of Wisconsin Press, 1972), p. 30.

31. Behl and Voigt, *Chronik,* p. 28.

32. For autobiographical elements see Daiber, *G. H.,* pp. 64–65; Heuser, *G. H.,* pp. 249, 252, 256; Hilscher, *G. H.,* p. 114; Jofen, *Das letzte,* pp. 130, 135, 141, 172, 237; and Margaret Sinden, " 'Marianne' and 'Einsame Menschen,' " *Monatshefte* 54 (1962): 312–13.

33. Cf. Behl, *Zwiesprache,* p. 127.

34. 7:939–40. See also Heuser, *G. H.,* p. 249.

35. Cf. Shaw, *Playwright,* pp. 44–45.

36. Cf. Henry A. Lea, "The Specter of Romanticism . . . ," *Germanic Review* 49 (1974): esp. 270–73.

37. Ibid., p. 278.

Chapter Four

1. Fechter, *G. H.,* p. 78; Guthke, *G. H.,* p. 73, and Furst, *Naturalism,* p. 66.

2. Hugh F. Garten, *Gerhart Hauptmann* (New Haven, 1954), p. 19.

3. Manfred Brauneck, *Literatur und Offentlichkeit* . . . (Stuttgart, 1974), p. 51.

4. See Hoefert, "G. H. und andere," in Scheuer, pp. 244, 249–50.

5. Cf. Cowen, *Naturalismus,* pp. 191, 197; Hilscher, *G. H.,* p. 145; Münchow, *Naturalismus,* p. 98, and Guthke and Wolff, *Leid,* p. 66.

6. The most vociferous critic in this category is Peter Szondi. See his *Theorie des modernen Dramas* . . . , 7th ed. (Frankfurt/M.: Suhrkamp, 1970), pp. 69–73, and Kurt May's opposing view in "Die Weber," in *Das deutsche Drama* . . . , 2 vols., ed. Benno von Wiese (Düsseldorff, 1968), 2: 163–65.

7. Hans Rabl, *Die dramatische Handlung* . . . (Halle, 1928).

8. Ibid., p. 38.

9. Brauneck, *Literatur,* pp. 50–81.

10. Hans Schwab-Felisch and Jobst Siedler, eds., *Gerhart Hauptmann*: *Die Weber.* (Frankfurt/M./Berlin: Ulstein, 1968), pp. 85–89.

11. Ibid., p. 93.

12. Ibid., pp. 103, 247, and Hilscher, *G. H.,* p. 152.

13. Alfred Zimmermann, *Blüthe und Verfall des Leinengewerbes in Schlesien* (Breslau: Korn, 1885); Alexander Schneer, *Über die Noth der Leinen-Arbeiter in Schlesien und die Mittel ihr abzuhelfen* (Berlin: Veit, 1844), and Wilhelm Wolff, "Das Elend und der Aufruhr in Schlesien," in *Deutsches Bürgerbuch für 1845,* ed. H. Püttmann (Darmstadt: Stein, 1845).

14. See Brauneck, *Literatur,* esp. pp. 54, 73, 78.

15. See Schwab-Felisch, *Die Weber,* pp. 163–175, and Behl and Voigt, *Chronik,* p. 34.

16. Quoted by Brauneck, *Literatur,* p. 152.

17. Klaus Müller-Salget, "Dramaturgie der Parteilosigkeit . . . , in Helmut Scheuer, ed., *Naturalismus* . . . (Stuttgart/Berlin, 1974), esp. p. 56.

18. Theodor Fontane, "G. H., 'Die Weber,'" in Schrimpf, ed., *Gerhart Hauptmann,* pp. 29–30.

19. Münchow, *Naturalismus,* p. 102.

20. Hilscher, *G. H.,* p. 146.

21. Cowen, *Naturalismus,* p. 196.

22. Mayer, *Hauptmann,* p. 45.

23. Quoted by Heuser, *G. H.,* p. 43.

24. Cf. Brauneck, *Literatur,* pp. 155, 156, 166.

25. Weigand, "Range," p. 322.

26. Guthke, *G. H.,* pp. 15–16; May, "Die Weber" in von Wiese, *Interpretationen,* p. 166; and Benno von Wiese, "Gerhart Hauptmann," in von Wiese, *Moderne,* p. 35.

27. See Brauneck, *Literatur,* p. 83.

28. Cf. Guthke, *G. H.,* p. 76.

29. Quoted by Alexander, *Studien,* p. 3.

30. Schwab-Felisch, *Die Weber,* pp. 174–75.

31. Quoted by Hilscher, *G. H.,* p. 183.

32. Leroy R. Shaw, *Witness of Deceit* . . . (Berkeley/Los Angeles, 1958), p. 81.

33. Quoted by F. A. Voigt, *Hauptmann-Studien* (Breslau: Maruschke & Berendt, 1936), 1:87. Cf. also Guthke, *G. H.,* pp. 92–94.

34. John J. Weisert, *The Dream in Gerhart Hauptmann* (New York: King's Crown Press, 1949), p. 63.

35. Cf. Alexander, *Studien,* pp. 79, 80, 85.

Chapter Five

1. Mayer, *Hauptmann,* p. 50.

2. Cf. Ludwig Büttner, "Gerhart Hauptmann: *Der Biberpelz,*" in *Europäische Dramen* . . . , ed. Ludwig Büttner, 2d ed. (Bonn, 1961), pp. 43–45.

3. For biographical influences see Behl and Voigt, *Chronik,* p. 25; Hilscher, *G. H.,* pp. 84, 164–65; Mayer, *Hauptmann,* p. 51, and Zeller, *Leben,* pp. 85, 345.

4. Weigand, "Range," p. 32.

5. Ibid.

6. Cf. Hilscher, *G. H.,* p. 172.

7. For a prolegomenon to such a study see Warren R. Maurer, "Gerhart Hauptmann's Character Names," *German Quarterly* 52 (1979):457–71.

8. Fechter, *G. H.,* p. 124.

9. Jofen, *Das letzte,* p. 133.

10. Quoted by Fritz Martini, "Gerhart Hauptmanns 'Der Biberpelz'" . . . , in *Wissenschaft als Dialog* . . . , ed. by Renate von Heydebrand and Klaus Günther Just (Stuttgart, 1969), p. 91. See also pp. 85, 92, 97, 100, 103, 104, 106.

11. Ibid., p. 90.

12. Cf. Gerhard Schulz, "Naturalismus und Zensur," in Scheuer, *Naturalismus,* p. 101.

13. See Büttner, "Hauptmann: *Der Biberpelz,*" p. 43.

14. Cf. Reinhold Grimm, *Strukturen* (Göttingen: Sachse & Pohl, 1963), pp. 8–43; Hans Joachim Schrimpf, "Das unerreichte Soziale: Die Komödien Gerhart Hauptmanns 'Der Biberpelz' und 'Der rote Hahn,'" in *Das deutsche Lustspiel,* ed. Hans Steffen, pt. II (Göttingen, 1969), p. 43; and Wolfgang Schulze, "Aufbaufragen zu Hauptmanns 'Biberpelz . . . ,'" *Wirkendes Wort* 10 (1960): 103.

15. Cf. Martini, "Biberpelz," pp. 92–93.

16. Cf. ibid., p. 110, and Schulze, "Naturalismus," p. 104.

17. Cf. Hilscher, *G. H.,* p. 173.

18. See Behl and Voigt, *Chronik,* p. 41, and Schrimpf, "Das unerreichte Soziale," p. 45.

19. Cf. Brauneck, *Literatur,* p. 162.

20. See Herbert W. Reichert, "Hauptmann's Frau Wolff and Brecht's Mutter Courage," *German Quarterly* 34 (1961): 439.

21. Quoted by Gerhard Fischer, "Der Naturalismus auf der Bühne des epischen Theaters. Zu Brechts Bearbeitung von Hauptmanns *Der Biberpelz* und *Der rote Hahn,*" *Monatshefte* 67 (1975): 226.

22. Cf. Hilscher, *G. H.,* p. 175.

23. J. Vandenrath, "Der Aufbau des 'Biberpelz,'" *Revue des Langues Vivantes* 26 (1960): 231.

24. Oskar Seidlin, "Urmythos irgendwo um Berlin . . . ," *Deutsche Vierteljahrsschrift für Literaturwissenschaft und Geistesgeschichte* 43 (1969): 126–46.

25. Ibid., p. 135.

26. Schrimpf, "Das unerreichte Soziale," p. 40.

27. Joseph Gregor, *Gerhart Hauptmann* . . . (Vienna, 1951), pp. 377, 379.

28. Hilscher, *G. H.,* p. 243.

29. Cf. Wolfgang Nehring, "Schluck und Jau . . . ," *Zeitschrift für Deutsche Philologie,* 88 (1969): 190.

30. For Hauptmann's indebtedness to this tradition and for the sources of his unusual names see ibid., p. 191; Garten, *G. H.,* p. 353; Gregor, *G. H.,* p. 377; Hilscher, *G. H.,* p. 242; Mayer, *Hauptmann,* p. 59; Felix A. Voigt and Walter A. Reichart, *Hauptmann und Shakespeare* (Breslau, 1938), pp. 23–25; Walter A. Reichart and Philip Diamond, "Die Entstehungsgeschichte des 'Armen Heinrich,'" in *Gerhart Hauptmann Jahrbuch* ed. by Felix A. Voigt (Berlin: 1936), p. 82; and Zeller, *Leben,* p. 353.

31. Cf. Guthke, *G. H.,* p. 254.

32. Nehring, "Schluck und Jau," pp. 205–6.

Chapter Six

1. Behl and Voigt, *Chronik,* p. 42.

2. Pascal, *From Naturalism,* p. 97.

3. See Zeller, *Leben,* pp. 108–12; Daiber, *G. H.,* p. 98, and Hilscher, *G. H.,* p. 235.

4. See Zeller, *Leben,* p. 123.

5. *Helios* (8:517–79), another fragment begun in 1896 is even closer to

Die versunkene Glocke in conception and content.

6. See 7:215, and Behl and Voigt, *Chronik*, p. 39.

7. See Garten, *G. H.*, p. 32; Hilscher, *G. H.*, p. 237; Weigand, "Range," p. 326; Warren R. Maurer, "Hauptmann's 'Die versunkene Glocke' and Ibsen's 'Auf den Höhen,'" *Monatshefte* 52 (1960) 189–93; Willy Krogmann, "Gerhart Hauptmanns 'Versunkene Glocke,'" *Zeitschrift für Deutsche Philologie* 80 (1961):158–64; and J. A. Walz, "The Folklore Elements in Hauptmann's Versunkene Glocke," *MLN* 16 (1901):98–100.

8. Weigand, "Range," pp. 326–27.

9. Cf. Jofen, *Das letzte*, pp. 222–23.

10. See Karl S. Guthke, "Gerhart Hauptmann und der Nihilismus," *GQ* 36 (1963):434.

11. Quoted by Wolfdietrich Rasch, "Hauptmann: '*Und Pippa tanzt!*'," in von Wiese *Das deutsche Drama*, 2:193.

12. Quoted by Daiber, *G. H.*, p. 141.

13. Cf. Lutz Röhrich, *Sage* (Stuttgart: Metzler, 1966), p. 28.

14. See Rasch, "Hauptmann: *Pippa*," p. 189; Guthke, *G. H.*, p. 105; and Behl, *Zwiesprache*, p. 224.

15. See esp. Hugo F. Garten, "Formen des Eros im Werk Gerhart Hauptmanns," in Schrimpf, *G. H.*, pp. 472–78, and Heuser, *G. H.*, pp. 100–54.

16. Cf. Rasch, "Hauptmann: *Pippa*," pp. 197–98.

Chapter Seven

1. See 7:817; Hilscher, *G. H.*, p. 257; and Mayer, *Hauptmann*, pp. 56–57.

2. Cf. Hoefert, *G. H.*, p. 30.

3. Hilscher, *G. H.*, pp. 256–57.

4. Quoted by Zeller, *Leben*, p. 115.

5. Cf. Guthke, *G. H.*, p. 99.

6. Cf. Zeller, *Leben*, p. 128, and Hoefert, *G. H.*, p. 38.

7. Quoted by Zeller, *Leben*, 129.

8. Ibid., pp. 126, 130.

9. Cf. Hoefert, *G. H.*, p. 102; Hugo Schmidt, "Hauptmann's *Michael Kramer* and Joyce's 'The Dead,'" *PMLA* 80 (1965): 141–42; and Marvin McMillan, "Influences of Gerhart Hauptmann in Joyce's *Ulysses*," *James Joyce Quarterly* 4 (1967):107–9.

10. Zeller, *Leben*, 132.

11. Cf. also Viktor Steege, "Michael Kramer," in Büttner, *Europäische Dramen*, esp. pp. 65, 80–81.

12. For autobiographical details see Charles R. Bachman, "Life into Art: Gerhart Hauptmann and *Michael Kramer*," *German Quarterly* 42 (1969): esp. 386, 388–89; Hilscher, *G. H.*, pp. 258, 260, 262; and Jofen, *Das letzte*, pp. 191, 196.

13. Bachman, "Life into Art," p. 384.

14. Cf. Helmut F. Pfanner, "Deutungsprobleme in Gerhart Hauptmanns 'Michael Kramer,'" *Monatshefte* 62 (1970):48.

15. Ibid., pp. 46, 47.

16. 1:1172. See also Guthke, *G. H.*, p. 92.

17. See Zeller, *Leben*, p. 143.

18. Hilscher, *G. H.*, p. 265.

19. See Behl and Voigt, *Chronik*, pp. 53–54; Daiber, *G. H.*, p. 208; Hans Joachim Schrimpf, "Rose Bernd," in von Wiese, *Das deutsche Drama*, p. 167.

20. Cf. Schrimpf, "Rose Bernd," p. 168.

21. Cf. ibid., p. 170.

22. See Sigmund Bytowski, *Gerhart Hauptmanns Naturalismus und das Drama* (Hamburg: Voss, 1908), p. 65.

23. See 7:730, 799; Müller-Salget, p. 58.

24. Cf. Guthke, *G. H.*, p. 102, and Schrimpf, "Rose Bernd," p. 184.

25. See Behl, *Zwiesprache*, p. 89.

26. Müller-Salget, "Dramaturgie," in Scheuer, *Naturalismus*, pp. 48–67.

27. Hoefert, *G. H.*, p. 44; Zeller, *Leben*, p. 178; and Gerhard Kaiser, "Die Tragikomödien Gerhart Hauptmanns," in Schrimpf, *G. H.*, p. 383.

28. For these and other background details see esp. Behl and Voigt, *Chronik*, p. 23; Behl, *Zwiesprache*, p. 119; Hilscher, *G. H.*, p. 297; Mayer, *Hauptmann*, p. 67; Jofen, *Das letzte*, p. 42.

29. See Behl, *Zwiesprache*, p. 119.

30. See also Guthke, *G. H.*, pp. 109–12; Mayer, *Hauptmann*, esp. pp. 15, 17, 30, 31.

31. See Karl S. Guthke, *Geschichte und Poetik der deutschen Tragikomödie* (Göttingen, 1961), pp. 260, 261–66.

Chapter Eight

1. See 7:1072–73; Behl and Voigt, *Chronik*, pp. 28, 33.

2. Karl S. Weimar, "Another Look at Gerhart Hauptmann's *Der Narr in Christo Emanuel Quint*," *Germanic Review* 34 (1959): 208.

3. Margaret Sinden, "Hauptmann's Emanuel Quint," *Germanic Review* 29 (1954):271.

4. For the novel's literary and historical background see Theodore

Ziolkowski, *Fictional Transfigurations of Jesus* (Princeton, 1972), pp. 99–106.
5. Weimar, "Hauptmann's *Der Narr,*" pp. 214, 219.
6. See Hilscher, *G. H.,* p. 289.
7. Cf. Hoefert, *G. H.,* p. 55.
8. Garten, *G. H.,* p. 41.
9. Cf. Hoefert, *G. H.,* p. 55.
10. Cf. Jofen, *Das letzte,* pp. 33, 78, 82.
11. See Behl, *Zwiesprache,* p. 111.
12. Fechter, *G. H.,* p. 134.

Chapter Nine

1. Cf. Guthke, *G. H.,* p. 129. Due to space limitations extended discussions of *Magnus Garbe* (written in 1914 and 1915 but not published until 1942) and *Die Winterballade* (1917) have had to be eliminated from this study. Two of Hauptmann's darkest tragedies, the former depicts the precipitous fall of two exemplary human beings: the strong and prosperous mayor, Magnus Garbe, and his beautiful, virtuous wife, Felicia. Unprepared, by the happy circumstances of their lives, to recognize and deal with evil—satanically personified in a papal inquisition—they are inexorably destroyed by it. *Die Winterballade* is a free, dramatic adaptation of Selma Lagerlöf's story *Mr. Arnes Treasure.*
2. See Behl, *Zwiesprache,* p. 216.
3. For Hauptmann's lifelong preoccupation with Shakespeare, see Felix A. Voigt and Walter A. Reichart, *Hauptmann und Shakespeare* (Breslau, 1938). This preoccupation is especially noticeable during the decade of 1926–36 in three works: *Shakespeares tragische Geschichte von Hamlet Prinzen von Dänemark in deutscher Nachdichtung und neu eingerichtet* [Shakespeare's Tragic History of Hamlet Prince of Denmark in German Adaptation and Newly Arranged (1928)]; the independent drama *Hamlet in Wittenberg* (1935), and the heavily autobiographical novel *Im Wirbel der Berufung* [In the Maelstrom of Vocation (1936)].
4. See Behl, *Zwiesprache,* esp. pp. 85, 216, 217.
5. Ibid. See also Hilscher, *G. H.,* p. 326.
6. Cf., Guthke, *G. H.,* p. 136.

Chapter Ten

1. For literature on Hauptmann's relationship to Goethe see Hoefert, *G. H.,* pp. 115–16.
2. For descriptions of Hauptmann's 1932 trip to America see Heuser,

G. H., pp. 67–91, and Klaus W. Jonas, "Gerhart Hauptmann in Amerika und England," in Schrimpf, *G. H.,* esp. pp. 425–27.

3. Behl, *Zwiesprache,* p. 25.

4. See Daiber, *G. H.,* p. 229; Fiedler, *Die späten Dramen,* p. 39; Guthke, *G. H.,* p. 150; Hilscher, *G. H.,* p. 398; Münchow, *Naturalismus,* p. 97.

5. Gerhard Schulz, "Gerhart Hauptmanns 'Vor Sonnenuntergang,'" *Germanisch-Romanische Monatsschrift* 14 (1964):281.

6. See Behl and Voigt, *Chronik,* p. 59; Mayer, *Hauptmann,* p. 71.

7. Schulz, "Vor Sonnenuntergang," p. 283.

8. Ibid., p. 286.

9. Alexander, *Studien,* p. 112.

10. See Zeller, *Leben,* p. 14.

11. Cf. Daiber, *G. H.,* p. 284, and Hilscher, *G. H.,* p. 471.

12. For the extensive literature on Hauptmann's indebtedness to earlier treatments of the material see Hoefert, *G. H.,* pp. 81–82.

13. Cf. Alexander, *Studien,* p. 112.

14. Cf. Rolf Michaelis, *Der schwarze Zeus: Gerhart Hauptmanns zweiter Weg* (Berlin, 1962), p. 270.

15. Evident also in such disparate dramas as *Magnus Garbe, Die schwarze Maske* [The Black Mask (1830)], *Winterballade,* and *Die goldene Harfe* [The Golden Harp (1933)].

16. Cf. esp. Michaelis, *Der schwarze Zeus,* pp. 298–99, but also Fiedler, *Die späten Dramen,* p. 122, and Alexander, *Studien,* p. 116.

17. Hilscher's descriptive term, *G. H.,* p. 473.

18. See Behl, *Zwiesprache,* p. 167.

19. See Hilscher, *G. H.,* pp. 478–79.

20. Cf. Fiedler, *G. H.,* p. 111 n. 146.

21. Michaelis, *Der schwarze Zeus,* pp. 266–67.

22. Alexander, *Studien,* p. 119.

23. Ibid.

Selected Bibliography

PRIMARY SOURCES

Das Gesammelte Werk. Ausgabe letzter Hand zum 80. Geburtstag des Dichters am 15. November 1942, 17 vols. Berlin: S. Fischer, 1942. Because of the limited time available to assemble this edition (approx. one year) and because the work involved was largely accomplished by C. F. W. Behl and Felix A. Voigt, the designation "Ausgabe letzter Hand" is dubious at best.

Sämtliche Werke. Centenar-Ausgabe zum 100. Geburtstag des Dichters, 15. November 1962. 11 vols. Edited by Hans-Egon Hass and continued by Martin Machatzke. Frankfurt/M./Berlin/Vienna: Propyläen, 1966–74. Although not a "definitive" or a historical-critical edition, this edition is likely to remain the most useful for some time to come. Indispensable for any serious scholarly work on Hauptmann.

Gesammelte Werke. 8 vols. Edited by Hans Mayer. Berlin: Aufbau 1962. Contains most of Hauptmann's best-known work (notable exception: *Die versunkene Glocke).*

Die Kunst des Dramas: Über Schauspiel und Theater. Edited by Martin Machatzke. Frankfurt/M.: Propyläen, 1963. Very useful compilation of Hauptmann's comments relating to this subject.

Die großen Dramen. Berlin: Propyläen, 1965. Useful one-volume anthology which ignores the early "family" tragedies.

Die großen Beichten. Berlin: Propyläen, 1966. Hauptmann's most overtly autobiographical works.

Die großen Erzählungen. Berlin: Propyläen, 1967.

Die großen Romane. Berlin: Propyläen, 1968. Includes *Quint, Die Insel der Großen Mutter,* and *Wanda.*

Das dramatische Werk. 4 vols. Berlin/Vienna: Propyläen, 1974. Includes all of the completed dramas but not the fragments or variants.

Italienische Reise 1897: Tagebuchaufzeichnungen. Edited by Martin Machatzke. Berlin: Propyläen, 1976. Important document for Hauptmann's aesthetic development after his turn from the more extreme forms of Naturalism.

146

English Translations

The Dramatic Work of Gerhart Hauptmann. Translated by numerous translators. 9 vols. Edited by Ludwig Lewisohn. New York: B. W. Huebsch, 1913–29. Contains thirty dramatic works and includes translations of all of Hauptmann's best-known plays from *Vor Sonnenaufgang* to *Veland.*

Atlantis. Translated by Adele and Thomas Seltzer. New York: B. W. Huebsch, 1912.

The Island of the Great Mother. Translated by Willa and Edwin Muir. New York: B. W. Huebsch and Viking Press, 1925.

The Fool in Christ: Emanuel Quint. Translated by Thomas Seltzer. New York: Viking Press, 1926.

Flagman Thiel. Translated by Adele S. Seltzer. In *Great German Short Novels and Stories,* edited with an introduction by Victor Lange. New York: Modern Library, 1952. pp. 332–62.

The Heretic of Soana. Translated by Bayard Q. Morgan. Introduction by Harold von Hofe. (New York: Frederick Ungar, 1958.

The Weavers, Rose Bernd, Drayman Henschel, The Beaver Coat, Hannele: Five Plays by Gerhart Hauptmann. Translated by Theodore H. Lustig. New York: Bantam Books, 1961.

Bauland, Peter. *Gerhart Hauptmann's* Before Daybreak: *A Translation and an Introduction.* Chapel Hill: University of North Carolina Press, 1978. Best translation of *Vor Sonnenaufgang* for modern American audiences; useful introduction.

SECONDARY SOURCES

Alexander, Neville E. *Studien zum Stilwandel im dramatischen Werk Gerhart Hauptmanns.* Stuttgart: Metzler, 1964. Demonstrates the unity of Hauptmann's oeuvre on the basis of a consistent (and largely pessimistic) determinism.

Bachman, Charles R. "Life into Art: Gerhart Hauptmann and Michael Kramer." *German Quarterly* 42 (1969): 381–92.

Behl, Carl F. W. "Die Magie des Elementaren." *Gerhart Hauptmann Jahrbuch* 1 (1936): 51–59.

————. "Die Metamorphosen des alten Wann." *Gerhart Hauptmann Jahrbuch* (1948): 95–116.

————. *Zwiesprache mit Gerhart Hauptmann: Tagebuchblätter.* Munich: Desch, 1949. Indispensable source for Hauptmann's comments on his life, times, and works.

————, **and Voigt, Felix A.** *Chronik von Gerhart Hauptmanns Leben und Schaffen.* Munich: Bergstadtverlag, 1957. Detailed, extremely useful chronology.

Böckmann, Paul. "Der Naturalismus Gerhart Hauptmanns." In *Interpretationen,* edited by Jost Schillement, 2:269–94. Frankfurt/M.: Fischer, 1966.

Brauneck, Manfred. *Literatur und Öffentlichkeit im ausgehenden 19. Jahrhundert: Studien zur Rezeption des naturalistischen Theaters in Deutschland.* Stuttgart: Metzler, 1974. Mainly devoted to the political circumstances surrounding and influencing the reception of *Die Weber.* Carefully researched.

Brescius, Hans Von. *Gerhart Hauptmann: Zeitgeschehen und Bewußtsein in unbekannten Selbstzeugnissen: Eine politisch-biographische Studie.* Bonn: Bouvier, 1976. Almost a collage of Hauptmann quotations (many previously unpublished) which afford an insight into the author's political views, especially during the period of the Third Reich.

Büttner, Ludwig. "Gerhart Hauptmann: *Der Biberpelz.*" In *Europäische Dramen von Ibsen bis Zuckmayer: Dargestellt an Einzelinterpretationen,* edited by Ludwig Büttner, 2d ed., pp. 41–62. Bonn: Diesterweg, 1961.

Chapiro, Joseph. *Gespräche mit Gerhart Hauptmann.* Berlin: Fischer, 1932. Valuable commentary by Hauptmann on his work.

Clouser, Robin A. "The Spiritual Malaise of a Modern Hercules: Hauptmann's *Bahnwärter Thiel.*" *Germanic Review* 55 (1980): 98–108.

Coupe, William A. "An Ambiguous Hero: In Defense of Alfred Loth." *German Life and Letters* 31 (1977–78): 13–22.

Cowen, Roy C. *Hauptmann Kommentar zum dramatischen Werk.* Munich: Winkler, 1980. Convenient summary of relevant facts and materials for all of Hauptmann's completed dramas.

————. *Der Naturalismus: Kommentar zu einer Epoche.* Munich: Winkler, 1973. Survey of German Naturalism; interpretations of several Hauptmann works.

Daiber, Hans. *Gerhart Hauptmann: Oder der letzte Klassiker.* Vienna/Munich/Zürich: Molden, 1971. Includes some previously unpublished material; presentation is marred by journalistic style.

Ellis, John M. *Narration in the German Novelle: Theory and Interpretation.* London: Cambridge University Press, 1974. A close analysis of the role of the narrator in *Bahnwärter Thiel,* pp. 169–87.

Emrich, Wilhelm. "Der Tragödientypus Gerhart Hauptmanns." In *Protest und Verheissung: Studien zur klassischen und modernen Dichtung.* Frankfurt/M./Bonn: Athenäum, 1960.

Fecher, Paul. *Gerhart Hauptmann.* Dresden: Sibyllen, 1922. Still useful older appraisal.

Fiedler, Ralph. *Die späten Dramen Gerhart Hauptmanns: Versuch einer Deutung.* Munich: Bergstadt, 1954. Remains a standard work on the dramas in question.

Furst, Lilian R., and Skrine, Peter N. *Naturalism.* London: Methuen, 1971. Good introduction to the European roots and spreading of the Naturalist movement.

Garten, Hugh F. *Gerhart Hauptmann.* New Haven: Yale University Press, 1954. Quick introduction to Hauptmann and his work but partly superseded by later German scholarship.

Gregor, Joseph. *Gerhart Hauptmann: Das Werk und unsere Zeit.* Vienna: Diana, 1951. Contains numerous errors of fact and distortions. Use with caution.

Guthke, Karl S. "Authentischer oder autorisierter Text? Die Centenar-Ausgabe der Werke Gerhart Hauptmanns." *Göttingische Gelehrte Anzeigen.* 228 (1976):115–48. In-depth appraisal of the strengths and weaknesses of the best edition of Hauptmann's work.

————. "Gerhart Hauptmann und der Nihilismus." *German Quarterly* 36 (1963):434–44.

————. "Gerhart Hauptmanns Menschenbild in der 'Familienkatastrophe' 'Das Friedensfest.'" *Germanisch-Romanische Monatsschrift* 43 (1962):39–50.

————. *Gerhart Hauptmann: Weltbild im Werk.* Göttingen: Vandenhoeck & Ruprecht, 1961. A landmark of postwar Hauptmann criticism also available since 1980 in a second revised edition.

————. *Geschichte und Poetik der deutschen Tragikomödie.* Göttingen: Vandenhoeck & Ruprecht, 1961. For discussion of Hauptmann in this context see pp. 252–66.

————. "Die Gestalt des Künstlers in G. Hauptmanns Dramen." *Neophilologus* 39 (1955):23–40.

————. "Hauptmann und Freud: Eine Arabeske über die Logik des Kuriosen." *Neue deutsche Hefte* 26 (1979):21–44.

————. *Wege zur Literatur.* Bern: Francke, 1967. Contains several important essays on the later (mystical) Hauptmann.

————., and Wolff, Hans M. *Das Leid im Werke Gerhart Hauptmanns: Fünf Studien.* Berkeley/Los Angeles: University of California Press, 1958.

Leid (suffering) more significant for Hauptmann's work than *Mitleid* (compassion).

Heerdegen, Irene. "Gerhart Hauptmanns Novelle 'Bahnwärter Thiel.'" *Weimarer Beiträge* 3 (1958):348–60.

Hertling, Gunter H. "Selbstbetrug und Lebenskunst in Gerhart Hauptmanns Lorenz Lubota und Thomas Manns Felix Krull." *Orbis Litterarum* 20 (1965):205–16.

Heuser, Frederick W. J. *Gerhart Hauptmann: Zu seinem Leben und Schaffen.* Tübingen: Niemeyer, 1961. Especially useful for biographical details.

Hilscher, Eberhard. *Gerhart Hauptmann.* Berlin: Verlag der Nation, 1969. Best comprehensive treatment by a Marxist scholar. An enlarged and revised edition available since 1980.

Hodge, James L. "The Dramaturgy of *Bahnwärter Thiel.*" *Mosaic* 9 (1975/76):97–116.

Hoefert, Sigfrid. *Gerhart Hauptmann.* Stuttgart: Metzler, 1974. Very useful biographical, literary, and bibliographical survey.

Jofen, Jean. *Das letzte Geheimnis: Eine psychologische Studie über die Brüder Gerhart und Carl Hauptmann.* Bern: Francke, 1972. Raises some provocative questions concerning the state of Hauptmann's psyche, but a simplistic technique and unsubstantiated psychoanalytical overkill vitiate many of the conclusions.

Klarmann, Adolf D. "Gerhart Hauptmanns Wirklichkeitserlebnis: Versuch eines Rückblicks auf das Werden des deutschen Naturalismus." In *Traditions and Transitions: Studies in Honor of Harold Jantz,* edited by Lieselotte E. Kurth, William H. McClain, Holger H. Homann. pp. 228–45. Munich: Delp, 1972.

Kluge, Gerhard. "Hanneles Tod und Verklärung: Studien und Vorstudien zu Gerhart Hauptmanns Hanneles Himmelfahrt." In *Literatur und Theater im Wilhelminischen Zeitalter,* edited by Hans-Peter Bayerdörfer, Karl Otto Conrady, Helmut Schanze. pp. 139–65. Tübingen: Niemeyer, 1978.

Krogmann, Willy. "Gerhart Hauptmanns 'Versunkene Glocke.'" *Zeitschrift für Deutsche Philologie* 79 (1960):350–61; 80 (1961):147–64.

Lea, Henry A. "The Specter of Romanticism: Hauptmann's Use of Quotations." *Germanic Review* 49 (1974):267–83.

McInnes, Edward. "The Domestic Dramas of Gerhart Hauptmann: Tragedy or Sentimental Pathos?" *German Life and Letters* 20 (1966):53–60.

Martini, Fritz. "Gerhart Hauptmanns 'Der Biberpelz:' Gedanken zum Bautypus einer naturalistischen Komödie." In *Wissenschaft als Dialog: Studien zur Literatur und Kunst seit der Jahrhundertwende.* Edited by

Renate Heydebrand and Klaus Günther Just, pp. 83–111. Stuttgart: Metzler, 1969.

————. *Das Wagnis der Sprache: Interpretationen deutscher Prosa von Nietzsche bis Benn.* Stuttgart: Klett, 1954. Sensitive interpretation of *Thiel,* pp. 56–98.

Maurer, Warren R. "Gerhart Hauptmann's Character Names." *German Quarterly* 52 (1979):457–471.

————. "Hauptmann's 'Die versunkene Glocke' and Ibsen's 'Auf den Höhen'" *Monatshefte* 25 (1960:189–93.

————. *The Naturalist Image of German Literature: A Study of the German Naturalists' Appraisal of their Literary Heritage.* Munich: Fink, 1972.

May, Kurt. "Hauptmann: 'Die Weber.'" In *Das deutsche Drama vom Barock bis zur Gegenwart: Interpretationen,* edited by Benno von Wiese, 2:158–66. Düsseldorf: Bagel, 1968.

Mayer, Hans. Hauptmann, 3rd ed. Velber: Friedrich, 1973. Emphasis on social criticism. Ideological bias.

Michaelis, Rolf. *Der schwarze Zeus: Gerhart Hauptmanns zweiter Weg.* Berlin: Argon, 1962. Defends later dramas as stageworthy. Ignores much secondary literature but provides some good, close readings.

Mühler, Robert. "Kosmos und Psyche in Gerhart Hauptmanns Glashüttenmärchen 'Und Pippa tanzt!'" In Robert Mühler, *Dichtung der Krise,* pp. 291–406. Vienna: Herold, 1951.

Muller, Siegfried H. "Gerhart Hauptmann's Relation to American Literature and his Concept of America." *Monatshefte* 44 (1952):333–39.

Nehring, Wolfgang. "'Schluck und Jau'; Impressionismus bei Gerhart Hauptmann." *Zeitschrift für Deutsche Philologie* 88 (1969):189–209.

Osborne, John. *The Naturalist Drama in Germany.* Manchester: Manchester University Press; Totowa N.J.: Rowan and Littlefield, 1971. Strong preference for Hauptmann's Naturalist dramas.

Pfanner, Helmut F. "Deutungsprobleme in Hauptmanns Michael Kramer." *Monatshefte* 62 (1970).

Rabl, Hans. *Die dramatische Handlung in Gerhart Hauptmanns Webern.* In *Bausteine zur Geschichte der deutschen Literatur,* vol. 25, edited by Franz Saran. Halle/S.: Niemeyer, 1928. Useful but somewhat simplistic analysis of the structure of *Die Weber.*

Rasch, Wolfdietrich. "Hauptmann: 'Und Pippa tanzt!'" In *Das deutsche Drama vom Barock bis zur Gegenwart: Interpretationen,* edited by Benno von Wiese, 2:187–208. Düsseldorf: Bagel, 1968.

Reichart, Walter A. "Fifty Years of Hauptmann Study in America (1894–1944): A Bibliography." *Monatshefte* 37 (1945): 1–31. Continued as "Hauptmann Study in America: A Continuation Bibliography,"

Monatshefte 54 (1962): 197–310. Includes references to numerous translations of Hauptmann's work and critical studies by American and Canadian scholars. Many items listed are in English.

————. *Gerhart-Hauptmann-Bibliographie*. Bad Homburg/Berlin/Zurich: Gehlen, 1969. Judicious selection of primary and secondary sources. Also lists reviews for many of the more significant monographs.

————. "Gerhart Hauptmann's Dramas on the American Stage." *Maske und Kothurn* 8 (1962):223–32.

————. "Grundbegriffe im dramatischen Schaffen Gerhart Hauptmanns." *PMLA*, 82 (1967):142–54.

————. and Diamond, Philip. "Die Entstenhungsgeschichte des 'Armen Heinrich.'" *Gerhart Hauptmann Jahrbuch* 1 (1936):59–87.

Reichert, Herbert W. "Hauptmann's Frau Wolff and Brecht's Mutter Courage." *German Quarterly* 34 (1961):439–48.

Rommel, Otto. "Die Symbolik von Gerhart Hauptmanns Glashüttenmärchen 'Und Pippa tanzt!'" *Zeitschrift für Deutschkunde* 36 (1922):385–404.

Scheuer, Helmut, ed. *Naturalismus: Bürgerliche Dichtung und soziales Engagement*. Stuttgart/Berlin/Cologne/Mainz: W. Kohlhammer, 1974. Nine essays on sociopolitical aspects in the work of Hauptmann and other German writers. Uneven quality.

Schlenther, Paul. *Gerhart Hauptmann: Leben und Werk*. Revised and expanded by Arthur Eloesser. Berlin: Fischer, 1922. Still a basic biographical study by one who knew the author well.

Schrimpf, Hans Joachim, ed. *Gerhart Hauptmann*. Darmstadt: Wissenschaftliche Buchgesellschaft, 1976. Excellent anthology of Hauptmann criticism from 1889 to 1971.

————. "Hauptmann: 'Rose Bernd.'" In *Das deutsche Drama vom Barock bis zur Gegenwart: Interpretationen*, edited by Benno von Wiese, 2:167–86. Düsseldorf: Bagel, 1968.

————. "Das unerreichte Soziale: Die Komödien Gerhart Hauptmanns 'Der Biberpelz' und 'Der rote Hahn.'" In *Das deutsche Lustspiel*, edited by Hans Steffen, 2:25–60. Göttingen: Vandenhoeck & Ruprecht, 1969.

Schulz, Gerhard. "Gerhart Hauptmanns 'Vor Sonnenuntergang.'" *Germanisch-Romanische Monatsschrift* 14 (1964):279–92.

Schulze, Wolfgang. "Aufbaufragen zu Hauptmanns 'Biberpelz': Ein Beitrag zum naturalistischen Drama." *Wirkendes Wort* 10 (1960):98–105.

Seidlin, Oskar. "Urmythos irgendwo um Berlin: Zu Gerhart Hauptmanns Doppeldrama der Mutter Wolffen." *Deutsche Vierteljahresschrift für Literaturwissenschaft und Geistesgeschichte* 43 (1969):126–46.

Shaw, Leroy R. *Witness of Deceit: Gerhart Hauptmann as Critic of Society.* Berkeley and Los Angeles: University of California Press, 1958.

Sinden, Margaret. *Gerhart Hauptmann: The Prose Plays.* Toronto: University Press, 1957.

————. "Hauptmann's Emanuel Quint." *Germanic Review* 29 (1954):269–81.

————. " 'Marianne' and 'Einsame Menschen.' " *Monatshefte* 54 (1962): 311–21.

Steege, Viktor. "Gerhart Hauptmann: 'Michael Kramer.' " In *Europäische Dramen von Ibsen bis Zuckmayer: Dargestellt an Einzelinterpretationen,* edited by Ludwig Büttner, 2d ed., pp. 63–86. Frankfurt/M.: Diesterweg, 1961.

Tank, Kurt Lothar. *Gerhart Hauptmann in Selbstzeugnissen und Bilddokumenten.* Reinbeck b. Hamburg: Rowohlt, 1959.

Voigt, Felix A. *Gerhart Hauptmann und die Antike.* 2d rev. ed. Berlin: Erich Schmidt, 1965. The definitive work on the subject.

————. and Reichart, Walter A. *Hauptmann und Shakespeare.* Breslau: Maruschke & Berendt, 1938. Traces the strong impact of Shakespeare on Hauptmann from his childhood through his "Shakespeare decade." A standard work by two of Hauptmann's most accomplished critics.

Weigand, Hermann J. "Auf den Spuren von Hauptmanns 'Florian Geyer,' " *PMLA* 52 (1942):1160–95; and 53 (1943):797–848.

————. "Gerhart Hauptmann's Range as Dramatist." *Monatshefte.* 44 (1952):317–32.

Weimar, Karl S. "Another Look at Gerhart Hauptmann's *Der Narr in Christo Emanuel Quint. Germanic Review* 34 (1959):209–22.

Wiese, Benno Von. "Gerhart Hauptmann." In *Deutsche Dichter der Moderne: Ihr Leben und Werk,* edited by Benno von Wiese, pp. 27–48. Berlin: Erich Schmidt, 1965.

Zeller, Bernhard, ed. *Gerhart Hauptmann. Leben und Werk: Eine Gedächtnisausstellung zum 100. Geburtstag des Dichters im Schiller-Nationalmuseum Marbach a. N.* Marbach/N.: Schiller-Nationalmuseum, 1962. Much previously inaccessible material on Hauptmann and his work.

Ziolkowski, Theodore. *Fictional Transfigurations of Jesus.* Princeton: Princeton University Press, 1972. Erudite study which places *Quint* in the context of a popular theme of Western literature.

Index